ENGLISH
CHURCH
ARCHITECTURE
THROUGH
THE AGES

By the same authors:

ENGLISH
ARCHITECTURE
THROUGH
THE AGES
Secular Building

ENGLISH CHURCH ARCHITECTURE THROUGH THE AGES

LEONORA AND WALTER ISON

ARTHUR BARKER LIMITED
5 Winsley Street London W1

The drawings of York Minster, All Saints'
Margaret Street, Old St Paul's Cathedral,
St Luke's Chelsea, St Pancras, St Mary-le-
Bow; the plan of Coventry Cathedral and
the plan and section of St Paul's Cathedral
are reproduced by kind permission of
Rupert Hart-Davis. They are from the book
Architecture in England — A Short History
by Jeffery Daniels, with drawings by
Leonora Ison.

Designed by Sasha Rowntree

Printed by A. Wheaton & Co., Ltd., Exeter

ISBN 0 213 76474 1

Introduction

For many centuries civilized man devoted his finest creative talents and much of his wealth to the service of his gods. The temples of Egypt, Greece and Rome are the greatest monuments of antiquity, and the most inspiring buildings of the Christian world are its churches.

Most pre-Renaissance churches ultimately derive from the Roman basilicas built in the fourth century under Constantine, the first Christian emperor. The classical temple was ritually unsuitable and too closely linked with pagan beliefs, whereas the secular basilica, or hall of justice, was a form of building adaptable for Christian worship. Approached through an atrium (cloister) and entered through a narthex (porch) the Christian basilica evolved as an oblong building divided lengthwise by colonnades to form single or double aisles flanking a wide and lofty nave, lit by a clerestory and ending with an apse, or tribune, where the altar was usually raised on a floor above a crypt containing holy relics. A transept interposed between nave and apse gave some basilicas a significantly cruciform plan. The circular or polygonal plan was often used for baptisteries but seldom for churches, except in the Eastern Empire. Its use for the Holy Sepulchre, Jerusalem, was recalled by the Crusaders churches (p. 41), and the magnificent domed churches of Byzantium were to influence the centrally-planned churches of the Renaissance.

Romano-British (– AD 420)

Christianity became a unifying faith throughout the Roman world in AD 313, too late to save the Western Empire. Threatened by the Huns early in the fifth century, Rome withdrew her legions from Britain, leaving it to the mercy of the pagan Anglo-Saxons, perhaps the most savage of Teutonic tribes, whose capacity for destruction was unlimited. As settlers they had at first little use for the temples, baths and basilicas of the Romans. Consequently, the only evidence of Roman Christian buildings is in excavated sites. Remains of a small church, an aisled basilica with a western apse, have been found at Silchester, Hampshire, and fragments of wall paintings once decorating a private chapel have been recovered in the Roman villa at Lullingstone, Kent.

Anglo-Saxon (AD 449 – 1066)

The Saxons were descended from forest dwellers whose natural building materials were wood, wattle-and-daub and thatch. It is therefore probable that the stone-built churches of the seventh century such as Reculver in Kent (p. 20), Bradwell-juxta-Mare in Essex, also Monkwearmouth, Jarrow, and Escomb in County Durham were the work of masons from Gaul, re-using stonework recovered from Roman ruins. Norman and later rebuildings must account for the disappearance of many large Saxon churches, but a splendid example survives at Brixworth, Northamptonshire, fully deserving Sir Alfred Clapham's assessment of it as 'perhaps the most imposing architectural monument of the seventh century surviving north of the Alps' (pp. 21–22). Hardly less interesting are the tenth century churches at Deerhurst, Gloucestershire, and Wing,

Buckinghamshire. As an accretive building, Deerhurst is an exemplar of Anglo-Saxon architectural development, exhibiting in its doors and windows the various forms of arch-head from the flat stone lintel, and the triangular head of two inclined stones, to the round arch of regular voussoirs. Continental influences on arch design can be studied at Wittering, Northamptonshire (p. 23), Worth, Sussex (p. 21), Stow, Lincolnshire and Great Paxton, Huntingdonshire.

The most impressive survivals of late Anglo-Saxon architecture are the tower-naves of Sompting, Sussex (p. 24), Barnack and Earls Barton, Northamptonshire (p. 22), and Barton-on-Humber, Lincolnshire (p. 22). The last two towers are ornamented externally with tiers of blind arcading, a crudely executed form of decoration derived from Carolingian sources such as the monastery gatehouse at Lorsch, Westphalia. Blind arcading also ornaments the small church at Bradford-on-Avon, Wiltshire (p. 20), a late seventh century structure re-edified after the Danish invasions.

The most notable churches built in England just before the Norman Conquest were Wulfric's Rotunda at St Augustine's Abbey, Canterbury and Edward the Confessor's Westminster Abbey (p. 20). The rotunda, built c 1050, linked the early seventh century east and west churches of the abbey, and its probable model was the great Romanesque rotunda of St-Benigne, Dijon, completed c 1018. Westminster Abbey, however, was the work of Norman masons and its design was modelled on that of Notre-Dame, Jumièges, near Rouen. Its building symbolized Edward's desire to Normanize England, a process rapidly completed by the Conquest in 1066.

Anglo-Norman Romanesque (AD 1066 – c 1160)

The dynamic energy of the Normans found expression in the arts of war, social organization and building. In AD 911, as marauding Northmen, they forced the French king to cede them the future Duchy of Normandy, and in 1066 Duke William made good by conquest his claim to England. By then the Normans were masters at building castles and churches in the Romanesque style of the European mainland, and they must have viewed with contempt the stagnant state of Anglo-Saxon culture, especially its architecture. By the end of William I's reign many important English monasteries had been rebuilt and new ones founded, all with buildings designed on the grandest scale to impress the native population with the majesty of the church and the power of their rulers.

Romanesque architecture originated in Lombardy around AD 800, with the rediscovery of Roman building methods, notably in constructing arches and vaults of masonry. The new style reached early maturity around 1000 in the great churches of Imperial Germany, France and Burgundy. There the important abbey of Cluny had become the source of far-reaching reforms, calling for a stronger emphasis on the outward expressions of faith. This required a continuity of services throughout the day, conducted with great solemnity, visual splendour and musical beauty, needing large, architecturally impressive, and resonant churches, with processional aisles and many side-altars for the worship of saints. As Cluniac ideas pervaded France and Normandy, they influenced the planning of most Anglo-Norman churches.

Any appraisal of Anglo-Norman churches must follow consideration of their prototypes in Normandy: Notre-Dame at Jumièges, begun c 1037, and St-Etienne, Caen, begun 1068. The elegant and economical bay design of St-Etienne (p. 50) with aisle and tribune arcades of equal importance, probably led to its adoption for the great churches of Winchester (p. 58), Norwich (p. 37), Ely (p. 11) and Peterborough (p. 59). But the severe and massive double-bay of Jumièges (p. 58) was the model for Westminster Abbey and influenced the design of Durham Cathedral, assuredly the finest of all northern Romanesque churches (p. 58).

The greater Anglo-Norman churches have cruciform plans, usually with very long naves containing the monks' choir, and relatively short presbyteries ended either by an apse with an ambulatory, as at Norwich (p. 25), or an echelon of apses, as originally at Durham (p. 26). The internal elevation is usually divided into three zones – an arcade open to the aisles, a second arcade, often subdivided, open to the tribune gallery, and a 'thick wall' clerestory with a wall passage screened by light arcading. The bays are sometimes single as at Peterborough (p. 35), paired as at Norwich (p. 37) or double as at Durham (p. 35). Massive piers of compound-shafted or cylindrical form, generally used alternately, support the boldly-moulded semicircular arches of the main arcades, and single shafts divide the tribune and clerestory arcades. The faceted cushion capital is general, although debased Roman forms are sometimes used, especially in the later buildings. Arch orders were plain at first, then simply moulded with rolls or bowtells, and later enriched with formal ornaments such as chevrons, frets, billets, cables and nailheads (p. 85). The grotesque beakhead and figure carving was generally reserved for such features as doorways and, in smaller churches, chancel arches (p. 66). Windows, small and round-headed, were recessed with internally splayed reveals in walls often decorated with a zone of blind arcading, often interlacing (p. 11). Although groined or ribbed vaults of stone were generally used to cover the small square compartments of the aisles or chapels, the wide and lofty naves had wooden ceilings, sometimes shaped to the profile of the roof trusses as at Ely (p. 79) and Peterborough. An important exception was Durham Cathedral, begun c 1093 and designed from the first to have high vaults formed with stone ribs and cells, the earliest of their kind in Europe.

The structural scheme of the interior was echoed by the exterior, the bay divisions being marked by broad flat buttresses rising to support the corbel-tables and parapets (p. 11). Towers, single or paired; gave prominence to the west fronts, and were invariably raised above the crossing, with windows lighting the choir. Crossing-towers are square and massive as at St Albans (p. 80) and Tewkesbury (p. 80), and seldom as tall and richly ornamented as at Norwich (p. 37). Lincoln's accretive west front is still dominated by the lofty arched recesses of its 'Gate of Heaven' built c 1090 (p. 30), and Ely was completed c 1160 with a sumptuously decorated 'westwork' composed of a tower flanked by short transepts (p. 28).

Although some Norman parish churches resemble small cathedrals, notably Melbourne, Derbyshire, and Hemel Hempstead, Hertfordshire (p. 43), more are modest buildings formed of two or three cells linked by arches, sometimes having a tower over the middle cell as at Stewkley, Buckinghamshire (p. 48), and Iffley, Oxfordshire (p. 48). Some are remarkable for the wealth of carved ornament lavished on their doorways and chancel arches, Kilpeck, Herefordshire (p. 66), and Iffley (p. 48) providing outstanding examples. Another small church noted for its rich ornamentation is Barfreston, Kent (p. 47).

Transitional and Early English Gothic

Arcades with pointed arches were probably introduced into England by the Cistercians, and their great abbey churches in northern England mark the process of transition from late Norman to Early English Gothic. Roche Abbey in south Yorkshire, built *c* 1160, has some claims to be regarded as the first English Gothic church (p.38). Although French influence is apparent there is little of the structural daring that pervades early French Gothic. Far more important is the eastern limb of Canterbury Cathedral, begun in 1175 after fire had severely damaged 'Conrad's glorious choir', a sumptuous late Norman work completed in 1114 (p.30). English and French masons were consulted and the rebuilding was entrusted to William of Sens, a French master. He built the choir and eastern transepts on a plan dictated by the surviving crypt and aisle walls, and he probably designed the retro-choir or Trinity Chapel, containing Becket's shrine, and the tower-like Corona, although William the Englishman built these parts later (p.29). The main arcade is lofty, the round or octagonal columns having plain shafts and Corinthianesque capitals supporting boldly moulded arches, mostly pointed though some are round. The triforium and clerestory, however, are low and elaborately arcaded so that the general effect is heavy. Canterbury's principal effect on English Gothic was through the decorative use made there of highly polished Purbeck marble, a practice almost certainly derived from the similar use of black Tournai marble in the cathedrals of Tournai and Valenciennes.

Canterbury's new choir influenced the partial rebuilding in 1190 of Chichester Cathedral's presbytery, and the building of a new eastern limb at Lincoln where work was begun in 1192 to a plan based on that of Canterbury (p. 29). The mixed use of round and pointed arches at Canterbury and Chichester was probably deliberate, the designers wishing to establish a harmony with the surviving Norman fabrics. At Lincoln an earthquake made complete rebuilding inevitable, and the eastern transepts of 1192 show little of Romanesque influence.

The twelfth century closed with work progressing on two important West Country churches, Glastonbury Abbey and Wells Cathedral. Begun *c* 1185, the vast cruciform church of Glastonbury was designed with a bay dominated by a high arch framing the arcade opening and the triforium screen (p.59), in effect a Gothic version of Oxford's late Norman scheme (p. 60). The rebuilding of Wells, a small cathedral served by secular canons, was also begun *c* 1185. Comparison with Roche Abbey suggests that the interior bay design of Wells, no less than its original plan, owed far more to Cistercian sources than to its Benedictine neighbour at Glastonbury. While the total effect of Wells is fully Gothic, it is in a style having little in common with contemporaneous work in France (p. 61).

By 1200 the work at Lincoln had progressed as far west as the great transepts. The bay design of St Hugh's Choir represents a considerable advance on the Canterbury work which was its model. The most remarkable feature is the high vaulting where a ridge-rib is introduced, divided in each bay into three equal lengths by carved bosses. These form stops for three branching ribs arranged asymmetrically to swing the intersecting vaults towards the east on the south side of the ridge, and towards the west on the north side, a contrivance allowing more effective lighting from the clerestory. Opinions vary as to the date of this 'crazy' vaulting, some authorities dating it after 1237 when the crossing tower collapsed. In their favour it must be said that the great transepts, presumably built later than the choir, have sexpartite vaulting with the transverse middle rib and cells dividing each bay of the clerestory zone (p. 62). Lincoln's nave dates from *c* 1225 and has a bay design similar to that of St Hugh's Choir, though wider (p. 39). The work is also more richly ornamented and the high vaults show a further advance in design, with the intersections framed, not by the diagonal ribs, but by extra ribs, or tiercerons, rising to meet short transverse ribs extending from the ridge-rib. This made it possible to introduce narrow splayed cells between those of the longitudinal and intersecting vaults, further improving the clerestory light and moving towards the development of lierne and conoid vaults (p. 75).

The classic Early English cathedral is Salisbury, begun *c* 1220 and completed in 1265, except for the central tower and spire. Planned for a virgin site, Salisbury has an aisled nave of ten bays, great transepts of four with an eastern aisle, an aisled choir of three bays, eastern transepts of three bays with an eastern aisle, and an aisled presbytery of three bays, square ended but provided with a double ambulatory opening east to a Lady Chapel of two bays (p. 38). Although Lincoln and Wells influenced some features, the interior has a very distinctive character due to the well-proportioned arcades with their compound piers of Purbeck marble. Even the squat triforium detracts little from the noble clarity of the whole design. The exterior, too, is an architectural conception of a very high order. Viewed from the north-east, the grouped lancets and gables of the Lady Chapel and flanking ambulatories form the base of a composition that builds up to the clerestory of triple lancets and the steep gables of the main vessels, all flanked with slender pinnacles and dominated by the magnificent central tower and spire added in 1365 (p. 29). The west front, flanked by small square towers with low spires, is divided by massive buttresses into three richly arcaded bays (p. 27). It is the latest and least successful of a series of Early English screen façades that begins with Peterborough and includes Lincoln and Wells.

The Norman cathedral of Peterborough, like Winchester, Ely and Lincoln, was planned with a 'westwork' in the Carolingian tradition. That at Peterborough was built between 1194 and 1210, in the form of a narrow western transept fronted by a great porch with three immense pointed-arched openings (p. 31). This Early English masterpiece was probably inspired by Lincoln's Norman west front, and influenced in turn the reconstruction work there in 1225. The middle recess of the 'Gate of Heaven' was heightened with a pointed arch rising into a wide face of tall arcading, designed to receive two tiers of figures and extending above the richly arcaded wings added to the Norman front (p. 59).

At Wells the impressive north porch is the ceremonial entrance (p. 27). The three west doorways are architecturally insignificant, allowing the west front of three bays, with the broad flanking towers, to form a vast screen decorated with arcading and tabernacles (p. 31). With its two zones, low beneath high, this richly articulated screen forms a setting for an elaborate iconographical scheme with 176 full-length statues, 30 half-length angels, and 134 small reliefs. Above the three tall lancets lighting the nave rises a stepped gable, containing niches with the Apostles below Christ in a mandorla. English Gothic sculpture reached maturity in this great west front at Wells.

Apart from the great transepts of York Minster, begun 1242, and the eastern parts of Beverley Minster, northern England has important examples of early English architecture in the ruined transepts and choir of Whitby Abbey, the choir of Rievaulx Abbey, and the beautiful eastern transept of Fountains Abbey This last probably inspired Durham's eastern transept, the Chapel of the Nine Altars, one of the last masterpieces of Early English Gothic. Begun in 1242, it was not completed until 1290, when a new phase of Gothic had developed employing large windows with Geometrical bar tracery, such as the superb double-traceried north window.

INTERNAL AND EXTERNAL BAY ELEVATIONS
Ely Cathedral presbytery, built *c.* 1240–50, Early English Gothic (late)

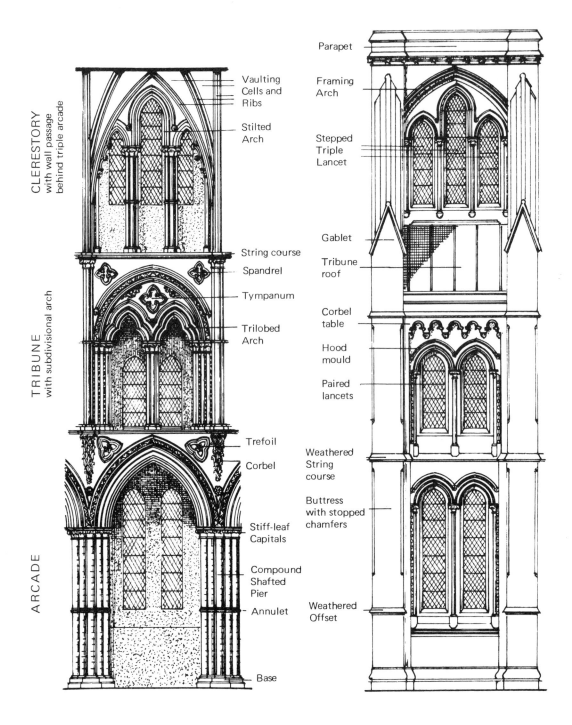

CLERESTORY with wall passage behind triple arcade

- Vaulting Cells and Ribs
- Stilted Arch
- Parapet
- Framing Arch
- Stepped Triple Lancet

TRIBUNE with subdivisional arch

- String course
- Spandrel
- Tympanum
- Trilobed Arch
- Gablet
- Tribune roof
- Corbel table
- Hood mould
- Paired lancets

ARCADE

- Trefoil
- Corbel
- Stiff-leaf Capitals
- Compound Shafted Pier
- Annulet
- Base
- Weathered String course
- Buttress with stopped chamfers
- Weathered Offset

INTERNAL AND EXTERNAL BAY ELEVATIONS
Ely Cathedral nave, built *c.* 1174–85, late Norman romanesque

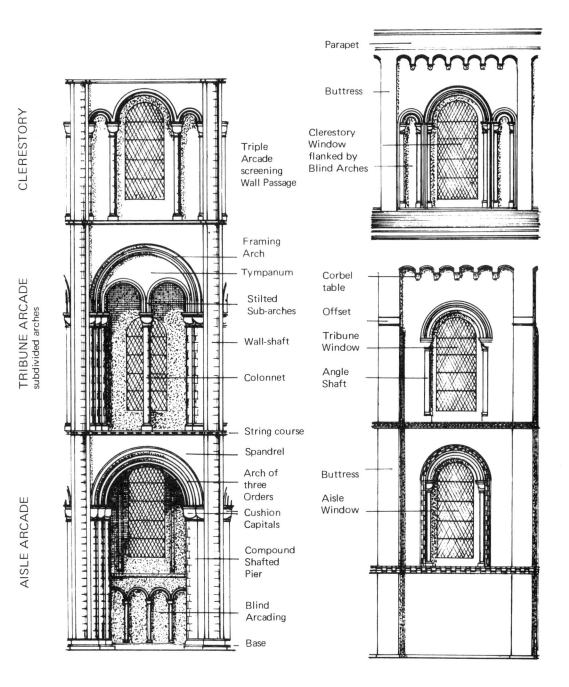

CLERESTORY

TRIBUNE ARCADE
subdivided arches

AISLE ARCADE

Triple
Arcade
screening
Wall Passage

Framing
Arch

Tympanum

Stilted
Sub-arches

Wall-shaft

Colonnet

String course

Spandrel

Arch of
three
Orders

Cushion
Capitals

Compound
Shafted
Pier

Blind
Arcading

Base

Parapet

Buttress

Clerestory
Window
flanked by
Blind Arches

Corbel
table

Offset

Tribune
Window

Angle
Shaft

Buttress

Aisle
Window

Decorated Gothic

At Chartres, about 1220, each bay of the lofty clerestory was built with two tall lancets paired below a large plate-tracery rose, providing a larger frame for a related expanse of stained glass than the biggest single lancet could accommodate. Later, at Reims, this innovation was perfected by eliminating some of the intervening stonework and moulding the rest to introduce small glazed spandrels between the heads of the tall lights, the foliated rose, and the pointed containing arch. This 'bar tracery' was introduced to England about 1244, when Henry III employed French and English masons to rebuild Westminster Abbey as a coronation church similar to Reims. Consequently, Westminster is not only important as a French-inspired masterpiece with specifically English features, but as a potent influence on the development of English Gothic.

Although Lincoln's Angel Choir, added in 1256–80, conforms in its general lines with St Hugh's Choir, the influence of Westminster is apparent in the rich decoration, notably in the triforium where the spandrels contain finely carved angels with extended wings (p. 75). The geometrical bar tracery is more elaborate than that at Westminster and the clerestory windows are duplicated by inner unglazed screens to form what is called 'double tracery' (p. 62). The great traceried east window goes far to justify English preference for the square end, against the elaborate polygonal chevet favoured by the French and used at Westminster. The nave of Lichfield Cathedral, built 1250–80, shows the influence of Lincoln and Westminster, the latter contributing the convex-sided triangular windows of the low clerestory (p. 63). Despite the Perpendicular tracery in some of its windows, Lichfield's presbytery is a late Decorated work, designed with a bay of two lofty stages. The triforium is replaced by a tier of blind lights related to the clerestory windows which are recessed in splayed arches, their reveals penetrated to link a passage, protected by a parapet, above the main arcade. Selby Abbey has a presbytery of the same style, although the clerestory windows are smaller than those at Lichfield (p. 39).

Except for its Norman transept towers, Exeter Cathedral is a late Decorated Gothic building, begun 1280 and completed about 1369 with little deviation in style throughout, although the windows exhibit a wide variety of geometrical and curvilinear tracery patterns (p. 32). The most magnificent feature is the elaborate stone vaulting, extending unbroken from the east end to the west. It is formed with longitudinal and transverse ridge-ribs, transverse arching ribs between the bays, diagonal arching ribs, and no less than four tiercerons. All the ribs are heavily moulded, and richly carved bosses ornament the ridge-ribs. York Minster's nave was built between 1291 and 1324 on the same vast scale as the Early English great transepts. With an internal width of 48 feet and a height of 98 feet, the general effect is very impressive although the late Decorated bay design of two stages has neither the charm of Lichfield nor the robust splendour of Exeter (p. 32).

The Octagon at Ely and the eastern extension of Wells are among the masterpieces of late Decorated Gothic. Ely's central tower collapsed in 1322 and the sacrist Alan of Walsingham, with his master-carpenter William Hurley, replaced it with a spacious octagon 74 feet across, perhaps inspired by that of the cathedral in Florence. The wide faces have lofty arches opening to the arms of the cruciform cathedral, whereas each narrow diagonal face contains a clerestory window of curvilinear tracery above an arch opening to the aisles. From this stone structure a truncated cone of timber framing rises to support a tall octagonal lantern, half turned so that its angles centre with the crowns of the arches below. Ribbed semi-vaulting of wood conceals the cone's framework and

a stellar vault covers the lantern (p. 76). The new Lady Chapel at Wells was built
c 1320, preceding the remodelling and lengthening of the Early English presbytery (p. 38). This work was completed with an ambulatory of complex plan,
having square chapels projecting north and south, and a hexagonal chapel for
relics opening to the octangular Lady Chapel. This arrangement produced an
interior of exquisite vistas, with the vaulting ribs spreading like palm branches
from slender clusters of Purbeck marble shafts.

The outstanding Decorated Gothic west fronts are at Lichfield, Exeter and
York. Lichfield's front was begun c 1280 and finished by 1327, except for the
twin spires that contribute effectively to its silhouette, so like that of the French
ideal cathedral façade. These apart, the front is really an arcaded screen for
sculpture in the Wells tradition, though without buttresses to distinguish the
nave from the aisles (p. 32). Exeter's west front of 1346–74 is a curious composition of two low stages, the lower one a rich 'image screen' (p. 32). York's magnificent west front was begun c 1289 and finished by 1345 except for the crowning
stages of the twin towers, which are Perpendicular but accord well with the
Decorated work below (p. 32). Lincoln and Selby have Decorated Gothic east
elevations of similar composition. Lincoln, the earlier, is more elaborate but less
felicitous than Selby which derives its effect from the varied and beautiful
tracery of its windows (p. 39). The cathedrals of Ripon and Carlisle, and the
ruined choir of Howden church also have fine east fronts of this type and period,
but the most sumptuous example is at York, a design of cold perfection completed c 1373, its central bay almost filled by an immense window of Perpendicular tracery.

Lincoln and Hereford have noble Decorated central towers, the last anticipating the tower added, with the lofty spire, to Salisbury in 1334–65. Both lofty
stages of the tower have four subdivided arches in each face, grouped in pairs
and finished with acute gables below rich diaper crestings. The polygonal
buttresses are dressed with gabled tabernacles and finished with pinnacles.
Behind these rise tall pinnacled turrets which, with the gabled lucarnes between
them, form a lively surround for the base of the octagonal spire, its surfaces
plain but for three bands of diaper ornament and some stringcourses (p. 29).

Perpendicular Gothic

Just as the Decorated style had germinated in Henry III's Westminster Abbey,
so did another royal work, St Stephen's Chapel in the Palace of Westminster,
begin the change to Perpendicular Gothic. The upper chapel, built 1331–60,
displayed all the characteristic features of the new style: panelled stonework
resembling window tracery; pier mouldings merging into the arches; rich
battlemented brattishing and a general emphasis on vertical lines. The first
splendid flowering of the new court style was at Gloucester where, in 1337–67,
the presbytery and crossing of the Norman abbey church were lavishly reconstructed to form a magnificent chapel enshrining the tomb of Edward II, then
venerated as a miracle-working martyr (pp. 40).   The new work was completed with an extremely elaborate lierne vault of stone, but the early fifteenth-
century cloisters introduced a new form of vaulting using semi-conoid fans
(p. 77). The earliest high vaults of this type are at Sherborne Abbey, Dorset,
where the presbytery was rebuilt c 1430–40 and the Norman nave reconstructed
with a new clerestory c 1475–90. At Sherborne the fans, though fully developed,
are formed with ribs prolonged to meet the longitudinal and transverse ridge-
ribs, producing in the centre of each bay a complex pattern of foliated triangles

13

(p. 65). Another high vault of very elaborate design, combining fans and lierne stars, was constructed *c* 1478–1503 over the Norman presbytery of Oxford Cathedral (p. 59).

Among the major works undertaken during the late fourteenth century were the rebuilding of the nave, main transepts, and cloisters of Canterbury Cathedral, the transformation of Winchester's Norman nave, and the completion of York's eastern limb. Henry Yevele's nave at Canterbury, *c* 1378–1405, is one of the finest late Gothic interiors, with the spacious elegance of a hall-church.

York Minster's choir shows a conservative taste, the bay design repeating that of the Decorated nave except for the decorative details and window tracery. Similarly, the bay design of Beverley Minster's nave, begun 1320 and finished *c* 1400, departs only in details from that of the Early English choir. Another great work completed with few departures from the original design was Westminster Abbey's nave, where work was first resumed under Yevele in 1375 (p. 62).

Royal master-masons were responsible for three outstanding masterpieces of the Perpendicular style: King's College Chapel at Cambridge, St George's Chapel in Windsor Castle, and Henry VII's Lady Chapel at Westminster Abbey. Henry VI's master mason, Reginald Ely, planned King's College Chapel, begun *c* 1443 but not finished until 1515. Congregational space, choir and sanctuary are contained in a single oblong vessel, wide and lofty, its immense length divided into twelve bays. Instead of aisles, there are low side-chapels between the great buttresses (p. 33). Every bay contains a great window divided by rectilinear tracery into two tiers of six lights. The east and west windows are even larger, having three main divisions each three lights wide, below traceried heads conforming with the four-centred arches that divide the bays and bisect the spreading fans of the splendid stone vaulting, added by John Wastell (p. 76).

St George's Chapel, Windsor, was begun *c* 1478 by Henry Janyns for Edward VI, and completed in 1528 by William Vertue for Henry VIII. The plan is basically cruciform with a very wide nave and choir, each of seven narrow bays with arcades opening to aisles linked by an ambulatory behind the square east end. The transverse oblong crossing opens to narrow transepts of one bay, each leading to a polygonal chapel. Small versions of these project north and south from the end bay of each aisle. The bay design shows all the extreme mannerisms of the late Perpendicular style, in the thinly-moulded piers and four-centred arches of the arcades, the attenuated shafts rising to the vaulting, the angel-crested panelling above the haunches of the arches, and the stiff rectilinear tracery of the windows. The aisles, crossing and side-chapels are fan-vaulted, but the nave and choir have extremely elaborate lierne vaults of remarkably flat pitch (p. 40). The west front is typical of the period, with an immense window below a flat-pitched gable, flanked by tall octagonal turrets with ogee-cupolas echoing those of the polygonal chapels that project from the aisles.

William Vertue and his brother Robert were responsible for that most marvellous of late Perpendicular buildings – Henry VII's Chapel at Westminster, begun 1502 and completed 1519. Although the plan is essentially conventional, it is treated in a most original way. The wide and lofty nave of four bays has arcades opening to aisle-like side-chapels, and the five sides of the apse open to small square chapels separated by wedge-shaped buttresses. The internal bay design has three zones, the arcade of four-centred arches being surmounted by a tier of richly-canopied niches resting on angels-corbels and containing figures. The large clerestory windows are divided by rectilinear tracery into three tiers of cusp-headed lights. Slender shafts, in groups of three, rise between the bays to support the wonderful stone vaulting, spanning 33 feet and of so complex a design as to defy description. The basis of its construction is strong transverse arches which are largely hidden by pendant fans. In addition there are semi-fans against the walls, and small pendant fans in the middle of each bay (p. 77). The exterior of the chapel is as lavishly ornamented as the interior (p. 35).

The Windsor and Cambridge chapels have ogee-domed turrets but no towers, although the latter was first intended to have a tall detached campanile. Something of its character informs the handsome central tower of oblong plan at Bath Abbey, built 1501–39 and designed by the Vertues. Bath's west front (p. 33) relates both to that of Winchester (p. 35) and St George's, Windsor. Perpendicular towers added to earlier cathedrals include the central towers of Worcester, Gloucester (p. 82), Wells (p. 82), Durham (p. 28), York and Canterbury (p. 82), also the western towers of Wells (p. 83), Beverley, York (p. 32) and Canterbury.

Gothic Parish Churches (Early English to Perpendicular)

Uffington, Berkshire, has a little-altered Early English church of cruciform plan, aisleless but having a crossing tower and a large two-storied south porch (pp. 44, 49). The austerity of its architecture contrasts with that of the grand Norfolk marshland church at West Walton (p. 54), where Lincoln's influence is apparent in the beautiful arcades and in the clerestory, arcaded inside and out. The noble bell-tower, standing away from the church, is a typical regional feature (p. 80).

The transition from Early English to Decorated is seen in the very beautiful church at Stone, Kent (p. 53), attributed with good reason to a Westminster mason. Two magnificent churches almost wholly Decorated in style are those at Patrington, Yorkshire (p. 49) and Heckington, Lincolnshire (p. 49), their cruciform plans expressed in equally beautiful though dissimilar elevations (pp. 45, 46). Norfolk, rich in lovely churches, has in Cley an outstandingly fine late Decorated building, left unfinished through the Black Death (p. 55).

In the prosperous times of the late fourteenth and late fifteenth centuries, rich merchants vied with nobles as benefactors in rebuilding, enlarging, or embellishing their parish churches. To this generous rivalry we owe many superb late Decorated and Perpendicular churches in the rich mercantile cities, and in the wool-producing and cloth-weaving communities of East Anglia and the western counties. The cathedral-like church of St Mary Redcliffe, Bristol (pp. 46, 51) was commended by Elizabeth I as 'the fairest, goodliest, and most famous parish church in England'. Hardly less impressive is St Botolph's, Boston, Lincolnshire (p. 49), with its famous 'Stump' rising 272 feet in height, while nearby Louth has a splendid Decorated church dominated by the most beautiful of all Perpendicular steeples (p. 81). Thomas Spring, heading Lavenham's rich clothiers, combined with the Thirteenth Earl of Oxford to build the magnificent new nave and tower of their great Suffolk church (p. 50), while three local families shared the cost of building the lovely Perpendicular church at Salle, Norfolk (p. 56).

East Anglia's Perpendicular churches are famed for their elaborate external decoration of flint flushwork (p. 50) and for their marvellous angel-decked timber roofs (pp. 78, 79), whereas the West Country churches are probably unexcelled for the splendour of their towers, often with elaborate coronals of perforated stonework, the tallest and most richly decorated being that at Taunton, Somerset (p. 83). Spires are as rare in the western counties as they are common in

15

Northamptonshire and Lincolnshire, the former county possessing noble examples of the broach spire at Raunds (p. 81) and Warmington, while Grantham, Lincolnshire (p. 81) has one of the finest and tallest spired steeples in England, a harmony of Early English and Decorated work.

Many large parish churches are accretive, preserving features from each stage of their development. That at Witney, Oxfordshire, is a large cruciform building, its late Gothic appearance concealing the Norman nucleus (p. 43). The magnificent Perpendicular church at Cirencester, Gloucestershire (p. 51), grew by additions and rebuildings to its present vast size, and Abingdon, Berkshire, has a church where only lateral enlargement was possible, so that its width exceeds its length (pp. 54).

Post Reformation to Late Georgian (c 1540 – 1830)

Henry VIII's Reformation, followed by the Act of 1545 dissolving all chantries and free chapels, extinguished any incentives to build more churches in a land well stocked with them. Many monastic churches were wholly or partly demolished, but parish churches were generally unharmed although despoiled of their imagery. Mary Tudor's return to Rome temporarily restored some splendour, but in 1559 Elizabeth's Parliament restored the Reformation, with the Prayer Book the only legal form of worship. Despite later onslaughts by Dissenters, the Anglican form of worship was little changed until the Tractarian Revival of the 1840s.

Church-building was largely confined to restoration and minor works during the reigns of Elizabeth and James I, but St Katherine Creechurch, London (p. 96), is an interesting Anglican church built under Laud's influence, its architecture combining the Gothic past with the Renaissance present. The outstanding Caroline church is St Paul's, Covent Garden (p. 96), built 1631 and designed by Inigo Jones (1573–1652) as a Tuscan temple dominating his Italianate piazza. Jones also began to transform Old St Paul's into a cathedral of Roman grandeur, giving its façade a magnificent Corinthian portico that was the wonder of its time (p. 97), but the Civil War brought his work to a standstill.

Charles II, and the Fire of London, gave Sir Christopher Wren (1632–1723) opportunities denied to Jones. Turning to architecture by force of circumstances, Wren's progressive mastery is seen in the successive designs for rebuilding St Paul's, from the first tentative schemes to the Michelangelesque grandeur of the 1673 Great Model (p. 98), and the evolution, from the eccentric Warrant Design, of the splendid cathedral that he began in 1675 and completed in his lifetime (p. 98). Wren also was responsible for rebuilding fifty-one of the City's churches, the variety of their plans, ingeniously fitted to awkward sites, testifying to his early love of geometry (pp 100-103). St Stephen's Wallbrook has the finest interior (p.100), but it is the superb steeples that most command our admiration, notably those of St Mary-le-Bow (p.102), St Bride (p.102) and St Vedast (p.102). In Canaletto's paintings we can recall the wonderful skyline Wren created by surrounding St Paul's great dome with a host of elegant steeples rising above the roofs of London.

Despite London's expansion, little account was taken of the people's spiritual needs until 1711, when Queen Anne's Tory government passed an Act for 'Building . . . fifty new churches of stone and other proper Materials, with Towers or Steeples to each of them'. This Act produced the Baroque masterpieces of Nicholas Hawksmoor (1661–1736) and Thomas Archer (1668–1743).

Besides St George's, Bloomsbury (p.109), Hawksmoor designed the three great churches in Stepney: St Anne's Limehouse (p.108), St George's Wapping, and Christ Church Spitalfields (p.109). Archer, having already proved his ability with St Philip's Birmingham (p.106), designed St Paul's Deptford and St John's Westminster (p.107).

Although fully appreciated today, these noble churches were soon to be derided by the Whig Palladians as 'mere Gothique heaps of stone'. Yet it was James Gibbs (1682–1754), a Tory architect trained in Baroque Rome, who created the ideal model for so many Georgian churches. His St Martin-in-the-Fields, London (p.110), a galleried basilica within a Roman Corinthian temple, crowned by a steeple worthy of Wren, inspired churches throughout the British Isles, the American colonies, and India. Similarly, his published designs for a circular St Martin's (p 110) influenced the building of several fine churches of this form, notably All Saints, Newcastle-upon-Tyne and St Chad's, Shrewsbury (p.110).

Although Renaissance churches now predominated, the Gothic seed lay ready to germinate, sometimes producing strange hybrids like St Peter's, Galby, Leicestershire (p.111). The charming Rococo-Gothic is seen in St John's, Shobden, Herefordshire (p.112), but the most remarkable Georgian Gothic church is St Mary's, Tetbury, Gloucestershire (p.112), its elegant interior curiously anticipating that of the new Coventry Cathedral. A Rococo-Gothic church at Croome, Worcestershire, has been attributed to Robert Adam (1728–92) who designed the neo-Classical church at Mistley, Essex (p.113), the form of its twin towers influencing Soane when he came to design his London churches in Marylebone, Walworth, and Bethnal Green (p.113). These were built after Parliament, in 1818, passed an Act granting one million pounds towards providing an indefinite number of new churches to be built wherever needed. John Nash (1752–1835), Sir John Soane (1753–1837), and Sir Robert Smirke (1780–1867), as architects to the Board of Works, advised the Commissioners appointed under the Act and shared in the building programme. A basic plan was specified – an oblong auditory accommodating a large congregation all in sight of the altar and sound of the preacher – but architects were allowed choice of style, and so 'the Battle of the Styles' was begun. James Savage (1779–1852) drew on Perpendicular sources for St Luke's, Chelsea (p.114), giving the nave a ribbed vault of stone properly supported by flying buttresses, this structural honesty prompting Sir Charles Eastlake, the Gothic Revival's first historian, to commend St Luke's as 'the earliest groined church of the modern revival'.

Some 'Commissioners Churches' have interiors where a 'Strawberry Hill Gothick' flavour is given by windows of cast-iron tracery and wide plaster ceilings with ribbed vaulting divided by panelled expanses. Even the scholarly Thomas Rickman (1776–1841) collaborated with an ironfounder to build, around 1813, some churches in Liverpool where cast-iron was used for the structural frame, the skeletal arcades and window tracery, and even for external details such as pinnacles. Later he used more orthodox materials for such carefully detailed Decorated Gothic churches as Hartlebury and Ombersley, Worcestershire (p.117), but his chief claim to fame is his *Attempt to Discriminate the Styles of English Architecture*, published 1819, wherein he established the terms 'Norman', 'Early English', 'Decorated' and 'Perpendicular'. Although Rickman was inferior as a scholar to Robert Willis, and as a designer to A. W. N. Pugin, Eastlake fairly questioned whether 'in his twofold capacity of a theorist and practitioner, he did not do greater service to the cause than either his learned contemporaries or his enthusiastic disciple'.

Victorian (*The Gothic Revival*) and Modern

Augustus W. N. Pugin (1812–52) was more than Rickman's 'enthusiastic disciple', he was the prophet of the true Gothic Revival. Publishing his *Contrasts* in 1836, he used his eloquent pen and rapier-sharp pencil to castigate the buildings and institutions of his time by comparing them with those of the Age of Faith. *An Apology for the Revival of Christian Architecture in England* appeared in 1842 with a frontispiece depicting all the churches he had been commissioned to design since the appearance of *Contrasts*. One of the first was St Chad's, Birmingham (p117), its rich furnishings thought by Eastlake to be 'as correct in form as any antiquarian could wish', although the building seems to confirm the unkind assertion that Pugin was always willing 'to starve his roof to gild his altar'. This is certainly not true of St Augustine's, Ramsgate, Kent (p117), of which Pugin wrote 'I have never had the chance of producing a single fine ecclesiastical building, except my own church, where I am both paymaster and architect'. Pugin's call for a return to medieval standards of life and art were heeded less by his fellow Roman Catholics than by the Anglicans of the Oxford Movement and the Cambridge Camden Society. Both groups agreed that auditorium-churches could not suffice for true Christian worship, and that buildings on near-medieval lines were essential for a revival of the full Anglo-Catholic ritual. Opposition there might be, but architects were waiting to build such churches and wealthy patrons were ready to pay for them.

The great scholar and artist-architect, W. R. Lethaby (1857–1931), classified Victorian Gothic architects as 'Softs' and 'Hards'. The former were facile imitators content to design stylistically correct buildings, whereas the latter were 'thinkers and constructors' ready for architectural experiment and concerned with structural honesty. The 'Softs' included the busiest of all Victorian architects, Sir Gilbert Scott (1811–78) and even R. C. Carpenter (1812–55), although the last was a medievalist whose fine taste is evident in St Paul's, Brighton (p.115). The hardest of the 'Hards' was William Butterfield (1814–1900) whose masterpiece is All Saints, Margaret Street, London (p.118). Building for permanency of decoration as well as structure, he used a vivid polychromy largely based on the natural colours of his materials, and much of his inspiration for this came from Italian Gothic sources. His style is eclectic although his details often relate to English Decorated Gothic. A similar taste for structural polychromy informs much of the work of George Edmund Street (1824–81) a 'Hard' architect of great gifts and wide knowledge whose artistic vocabulary was enriched by his studies of Gothic art in Spain and Italy. One of his finest churches in London is St Mary Magdalene, Paddington (p.115) but even more impressive is the noble Catalan-inspired St John-the-Divine, Kennington.   William Burges (1827–81) was a 'Hard' architect with astonishing powers of design, whose medieval obsession led him to draw on vellum in the style of Villard de Honnecourt (c 1230). The cathedral-like nave of St Michael's, Brighton (p.119), is a perfect example of his Early French inspiration.

The earlier works of John Loughborough Pearson (1817–97) were less influential than the buildings of Butterfield and Street, but the impact of his later churches was widespread and long lasting. Perhaps best known for his Early English cathedral at Truro (p.121), Pearson's masterpiece is the superb church of St Augustine, Kilburn, London (p.119). George Gilbert Scott, junior (1839–97), a finer artist than his more successful father, formed his own beautiful style on the study of Perpendicular churches, hitherto despised as decadent. His work influenced, in turn, that of George Frederick Bodley (1827–1907) and John Dando Sedding (1838–91), the latter designing, in partnership with Henry Wilson (1864–1934), churches combining the neo-Perpendicular with Art Nouveau.

'The heir to Butterfield and Bodley' was Sir John Betjeman's description of Sir Ninian Comper (1864–1960), the architect-craftsman whose work is at once the consummation of the Gothic Revival and its swan song. His early purely Gothic style is seen to perfection in St Cyprian's, Marylebone, London, whereas his later theory of 'unity by inclusion' produced his masterpiece in St Mary's, Wellingborough, Northamptonshire (p.120), its noble Perpendicular Gothic interior resplendent with painted and gilded Renaissance fittings, blended with an effect which Laud would surely have appreciated. Comper's work has been denigrated by at least one critic, but many will prefer it to non-stylistic churches such as St Andrew's, Roker, Durham (p.120), or the German-inspired one at Eltham, London (p.120).

Epilogue

Despite the spread of agnosticism and atheism, and a continuing decline in church-going, the twentieth century has already witnessed the building of five new cathedrals in England, two of them at Liverpool having been begun on a scale rivalling that of St Peter's, Rome. Except for their purpose, to provide a House of God where he can be worshipped with fitting ceremony by a great congregation, these new cathedrals have little in common for each represents a plan and a style which the architect and his patrons believed best suited to that purpose (pp.122, 4).

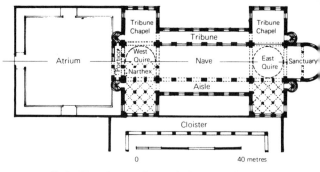

3 St-Ricquier, conjectural plan showing ground and tribune levels

1 The Carolingian Abbey Church of St-Ricquier (Centula), from a 17th century engraving

Right
2 BRADFORD-ON-AVON, WILTS
A small four-cell church of late seventh century date, re-edified in the tenth century (see figure 4 for plan). The blind arcading shows Carolingian influence

Left
4
Edward the Confessor's Westminster Abbey, as depicted in the Bayeux Tapestry

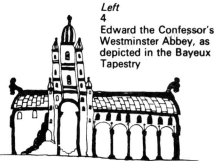

Right
6 MONKWEAR-MOUTH, CO. DURHAM
The original two-storied west porch of this church, built *c* 674, was heightened in the tenth century to form a tower. The time-worn figure carved in the stonework of the third stage is probably the oldest surviving example of English sculptural decoration on a large scale

Left
5 RECULVER, KENT
The ruins, looking west, showing the exposed foundations of the original four-cell cruciform church built *c* 670, and the later Saxon porticus surrounding the nave. The surviving west towers are Norman

Left
7 WING, BUCKS
The polygonal apse of this largely tenth century church is simply decorated with blind arcading allied to that on the tower-naves of Barton-on-Humber and Earls Barton

Romano-British and Anglo-Saxon

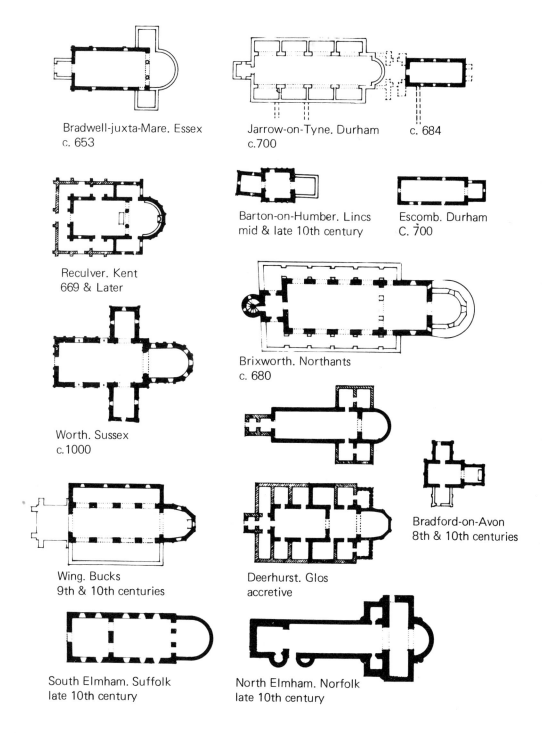

Bradwell-juxta-Mare. Essex
c. 653

Jarrow-on-Tyne. Durham   c. 684
c.700

Reculver. Kent
669 & Later

Barton-on-Humber. Lincs
mid & late 10th century

Escomb. Durham
C. 700

Worth. Sussex
c.1000

Brixworth. Northants
c. 680

Wing. Bucks
9th & 10th centuries

Deerhurst. Glos
accretive

Bradford-on-Avon
8th & 10th centuries

South Elmham. Suffolk
late 10th century

North Elmham. Norfolk
late 10th century

8 Comparative plans to a uniform scale of twelve Anglo-Saxon churches, their dates ranging from the seventh century to the eleventh

9 BARTON-ON-HUMBER, LINCS

The fore-nave and central tower-nave survive
from this three-cell church (see figure 4 for plan).
The blind arcading on the late tenth century
tower crudely reflects the influence of Carolingian
decoration such as that on the monastery
gatehouse at Lorsch, near Mainz

Right
10 EARLS BARTON, NORTHANTS

Originally dominating
a fort, this largest and
finest of Late Saxon
tower-naves has three
stages, each dressed
with long-and-short
quoins and decorated
with stone pilaster-
strips or lesenes,
linked by semicircular,
triangular and
X-shaped motifs. The
low top stage
contains open
arcading resting on
cinctured baluster-
shafts

11 BRIXWORTH, NORTHANTS

This largest and most important surviving
Anglo-Saxon church was built *c* 675 (see figure
4 for plan). In the side walls of the nave are wide
arches formed with two rings of re-used Roman
bricks, originally open to compartmented aisles
which were later divided into porticus. The
pointed chancel arch replaced the original
three-bay arcade, its form reflected in the east
wall where the middle arch opened to a
polygonal apse

Right
12 BRADFORD-ON-AVON, WILTS

The small but lofty nave has simply moulded
arches opening north and south to porticus, and
east to the square chancel. The carved angels
survive from a rood which is depicted restored in
a simple form (copied from one at Romsey) but
might have been more elaborate and partly
modelled in stucco

14 MONKWEARMOUTH, CO. DURHAM
The tunnel-vaulted porch of *c* 674 has a
remarkable doorway, its moulded arch of
voussoirs resting on shaped and panelled
imposts, above short turned shafts placed in
lateral pairs on high pedestals, their return faces
curiously carved with intertwined snakes

13 WITTERING, NORTHANTS
Continental Romanesque developments are
reflected in this late tenth century chancel arch, a
work of cyclopean scale and powerful effect. The
same combination of raised band and roll
moulding was used with greater refinement in the
crossing arches at Stow, Lincs

15 REPTON, DERBYS
The Late Saxon crypt is architecturally more
sophisticated than that at Wing, having an
orderly arrangement of vaulted compartments
divided by arches resting on four columns with
spirally-cinctured shafts, and responds with
panelled shafts

16 BREAMORE, HANTS
The south porticus arch of *c*1000 has cable-
bordered imposts and an arch with an incised
inscription. This, translatable as 'Here is made
manifest the Covenant which', was probably
continued on the arches of the chancel and north
porticus

17 JARROW, CO. DURHAM
This small church, built *c* 685, retains high up in its south wall of squared masonry, three of the original small windows, each with an arched head cut from a single block of stone

18 WORTH, SUSSEX
The nave windows have two openings, their arched heads resting centrally on a shaped abacus above an entasised baluster-shaft

19 BARNACK, NORTHANTS
The early eleventh century west tower contains windows with triangular and semicircular arched heads, the latter having spandrels carved with birds

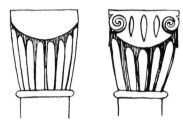

20
The south face of this tower-nave contains, in the lofty first stage, a pair of cruciform lights recessed in openings framed by segmental-arched heads resting on cinctured baluster-shafts

21 GREAT HALE, LINCS
Late Saxon proto-Romanesque capitals

23 SOMPTING, SUSSEX
Two sections of a ninth century stone frieze, carved with plaited foliage, re-used to form a piscina-head

22 DEERHURST, GLOS
A ninth century animal-head stone corbel

24 ST ANDREW AUCKLAND, CO. DURHAM
The richly carved base and shaft of an early ninth century cross

25 MELBURY BUBB, DORSET
A font of *c* 900

26 SOMPTING, SUSSEX
This simply decorated tower of *c* 1000 finishes with a gable on each face below a diagonally-placed pyramidal spire, forming a 'Rhenish Helm'

Cathedrals and Monasteries: Plans

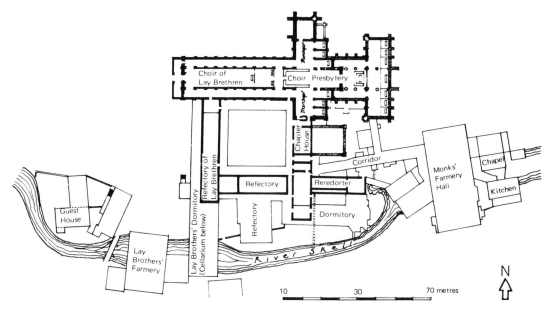

1 FOUNTAINS, YORKS

Fountains Abbey was founded by monks seceding from the Benedictine Abbey of York. In 1133 they were received into the Cistercian order and Fountains were designated a daughterhouse of Clairvaux which sent a monk, Geoffrey d'Annai, to supervise the new buildings. The plan shows the original Norman layout of the abbey, built between 1140–50, together with outlines of the extensive Gothic additions made during the thirteenth–fifteenth centuries. The last addition to the church was the splendid north transept tower, an adjunct originally proscribed by this once austere order

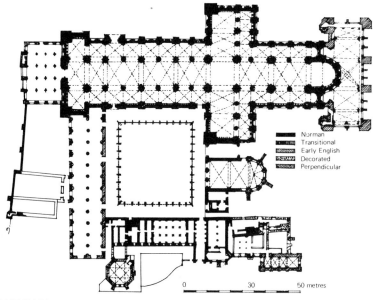

2 DURHAM

The great Norman cathedral is shown in its original plan form, with the later additions of the Late Norman Galilee, or Lady Chapel, at the west end, and the Early English eastern transept, or Chapel of the Nine Altars. The Benedictine monastery buildings, south of the cathedral, range in date from the twelfth–fourteenth centuries

25

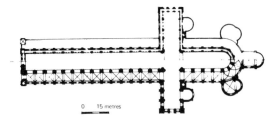

4 NORWICH, NORFOLK

The cathedral, attached to a great Benedictine monastery, has preserved to a remarkable degree its original plan of 1096. The upper half has been drawn to show the 'thick wall' clerestory passage extending round the interior, a typical feature of many great Norman churches

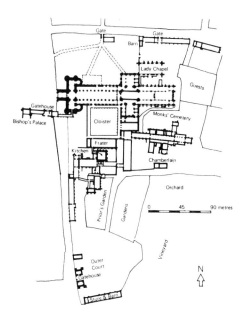

3 ELY, CAMBS

A plan showing the extensive buildings of this great Benedictine monastery as they existed at the time of the Dissolution. The interior of the church, now Ely Cathedral, is shown with its original monastic arrangement, the monks choir being placed in the Octagon, east of the rood loft

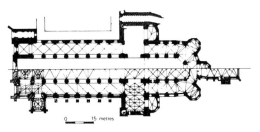

5 GLOUCESTER

The plan of this Benedictine monastery church, now a cathedral, is basically similar to that of Norwich, although the general design of the building was markedly different. The upper half shows the original plan of the Norman church, begun 1089, whereas the lower half shows how it was greatly transformed, in the Early Perpendicular style, after 1337

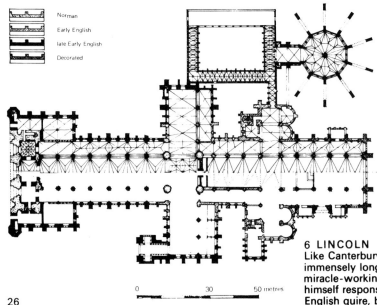

Norman

Early English

late Early English

Decorated

6 LINCOLN

Like Canterbury, Lincoln Cathedral owes its immensely long and transepted eastern arm to a miracle-working shrine, that of St Hugh, himself responsible for building the Early English quire, begun in 1192 on a plan similar to that of Canterbury's quire. The chevet originally intended was, however, replaced by t beautiful Angel Quire, begun in 1256

26

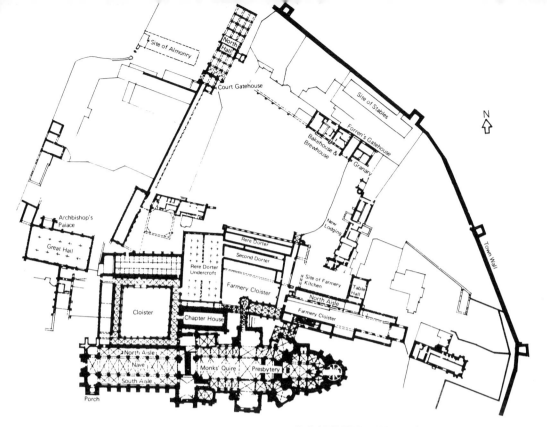

7 CANTERBURY, KENT

The cathedral is unusual in having a nave of only nine bays, a Perpendicular rebuilding on Norman foundations, and a Late Norman and Early Gothic eastern arm of vast size, due to its having contained the shrine of St Thomas of Canterbury. The buildings of the Benedictine monastery were placed, unusually, on the north side of the cathedral, occupying a very large area extending up to the city wall

Below
8 SALISBURY, WILTS

The classical simplicity of Salisbury's plan, its great length broken by main and secondary transepts, is of a piece with the cool perfection of its Early English architecture. The cathedral was begun on a virgin site in 1220 and completed by 1258, except for the famous spire, added *c* 1334

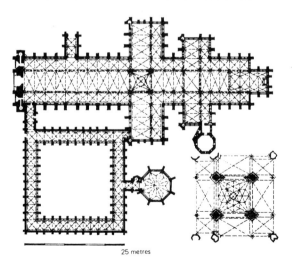

25 metres

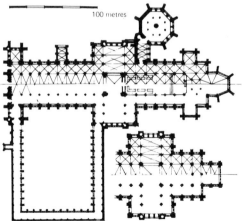

100 metres

9 WELLS, SOMERSET

The first mature Early English cathedral, Wells was begun *c* 1186 and virtually completed by 1240. The inset plan shows the original form and relatively small size of the choir, the first part of the church to be built, before it was extended and reconstructed in the Decorated style between *c* 1293 and *c* 1330

Cathedrals and Monasteries: Aerial Views

1 DURHAM

The grandest Romanesque church in Europe, Durham Cathedral was begun *c* 1093 and completed *c* 1140. The Galilee, projecting from the west front, is Late Norman, the eastern transept, or Chapel of the Nine Altars, is Early English to Decorated, and the central tower is Perpendicular. Except for the Norman chapter-house and the undercroft of the south range, the Benedictine monastery buildings are Gothic of the thirteenth and fourteenth centuries

2 TEWKESBURY, GLOS

Belonging to a Benedictine abbey refounded in 1092, this great church was built to a plan closely related to that of nearby Gloucester (see page 66). Except for the short eastern arm with its chevet of polygonal chapels, largely rebuilt in the fourteenth century, the exterior retains its Norman aspect, dominated by such features as the great arch of the west front, the arcaded clerestory, and the massive Late Norman central tower

3 ELY, CAMBS

The great Norman abbey church, now cathedral, was begun *c* 1080 on a plan closely related to that of Winchester, and brought to completion with the transept-flanked west tower about 1190. Its original appearance was greatly changed by the addition of the Early English Galilee Porch and by the lengthening of the eastern arm with a rich Early English retrochoir. The magnificent central Octagon was built in the Decorated style to replace the Norman tower which collapsed in 1322, and the exceptionally large Lady Chapel, north-east of the north transept, was added about this time. The lofty lantern of the west tower was raised early in the fifteenth century

4 CANTERBURY, KENT
The extensive eastern parts of this great cathedral are largely twelfth century Gothic and partly Late Norman, whereas the magnificent central tower and its flanking transepts, the splendid nave, and the south-west tower are all Perpendicular works of the late fourteenth and early fifteenth centuries

5 LINCOLN
The developing styles of Gothic architecture can be seen in the Early English transepts and choir, the later Early English nave, the beautiful Decorated Gothic retrochoir, known as the Angel choir, and the Perpendicular Gothic towers, those of the west front raised above Late Norman shafts

6 SALISBURY, WILTS
In many ways the most perfect and uniform of Early English cathedrals, its stylistic harmony unimpaired by the magnificent Decorated Gothic tower and spire added *c* 1334. The cloisters, which are the largest in England, and the octagonal chapter house, are early Decorated works of the late thirteenth century

The Greater Churches: Exteriors
Norman to Perpendicular Gothic

1 CANTERBURY CATHEDRAL, KENT
An early manuscript view of the Norman
cathedral in *c* 1164, after the lavish rebuilding of
its eastern limb. The paired towers at the east and
west ends, and the central lantern tower, called
the Angel Steeple, suggests a building closely
resembling the great Imperial cathedrals of the
Rhineland

3 TEWKESBURY ABBEY, GLOS
The Norman west front of *c* 1100 is dominated by
a giant arched recess, originally of seven orders,
now framing a 'Perpendicular' window of 1687.
The small turrets of two arcaded stages were
substituted for the large western towers
originally intended

2 LINCOLN CATHEDRAL
The monumental 'Gate of Heaven' with its five
stepped arches is an Early Norman masterpiece of
c 1090. It was embellished with carvings and a
tier of interlacing arcading in *c* 1150, when the
middle stages of the towers were added. The vast
arcaded screen extending the Norman front is an
Early English work of *c* 1250, and the tall upper
stages of the towers are late Perpendicular

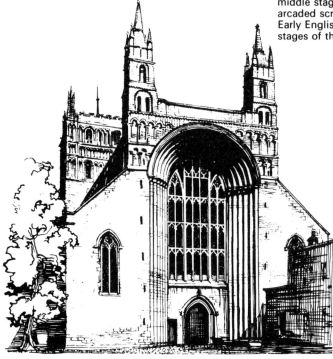

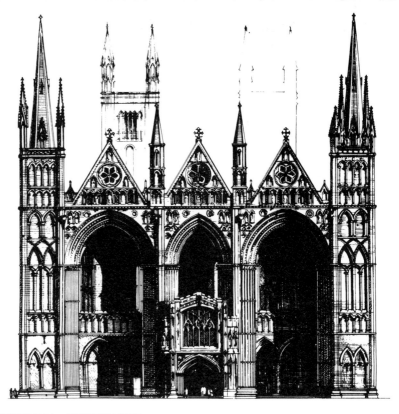

4 PETERBOROUGH CATHEDRAL, NORTHANTS
This remarkable and unique west front, built 1194–1210, is virtually an Early English version of the 'Gate of Heaven' motif, here forming a lofty open porch entered by three huge and richly moulded arches, crowned with gables and flanked by slender towers. The Perpendicular enclosed porch, projecting from the relatively narrow middle arch, was added in *c* 1375

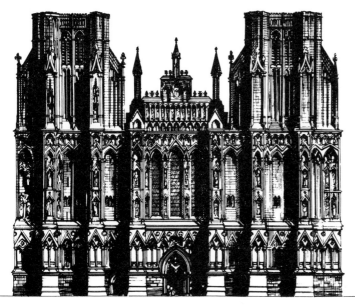

5 WELLS CATHEDRAL, SOMERSET
The west front with its flanking towers, probably designed by Adam Lock and built *c* 1220–33, was conceived as a rich architectural setting for an elaborate iconographical display of sculpture, a veritable 'Bible in Stone'. The upper stages of the towers, late Perpendicular works designed by William Wynford, were added later, the south in 1365 and the north in 1410

6 LICHFIELD CATHEDRAL, STAFFS

The use of successive tiers of niches and gabled arcading intended to house carved figures was here applied to a twin-towered front of the Decorated period, built c 1294–1327. Most of the figures are Victorian and the geometrical tracery of the great west window is a seventeenth century replacement of curvilinear work more in keeping with the cusped panelling of the nave gable

7 EXETER CATHEDRAL, DEVON

The highly ornate sculptural screen, probably designed by William Joy and built c 1370, projects well forwards of the true west front, its truncated triangular face crowned with battlements and containing a magnificent window of geometrical tracery, dominated by a great rose ringed with foliated circles

8 YORK MINSTER

The twin-towered west front is a magnificent and harmonious composition, although the lower stages of the towers are early Decorated, with geometrical tracery, and the great west window is a superb example of late Decorated curvilinear tracery set beneath a Perpendicular gable. The upper stages of the towers are also Perpendicular, but the ogee gables of the belfry windows accord happily with the rest of the front

9 SELBY ABBEY, YORKS

The east elevation of the choir, built 1280–1340, is a very beautiful Decorated Gothic example of the typically English square end, resulting in a composition first fully developed in the Angel Choir at Lincoln. Here, interest is concentrated on the rich tracery of the windows. Curvilinear tracery of great beauty fills the great east window, while that in the gable is reticulated as is the south aisle window, whereas the north aisle window is geometrical

10 BATH ABBEY, SOMERSET

This late Perpendicular church, begun 1499, has a west front of similar composition to that of Winchester. The decoration, however, is much less mechanical, for instead of stiff panelling there is the delightful conceit of carved angels filling the tympanum of the battlemented gable over the great west window, while more angels ascend and descend the 'Jacob's Ladders' on the shafts of the octagonal turrets

11 KING'S COLLEGE CHAPEL, CAMBRIDGE

This splendid chapel, completed in 1515, is a single vessel of great length, width and height, having east and west elevations of similar design. Each has an immense window of rectilinear tracery, below a low-pitched gable crested with perforated battlements, and between octagonal angle turrets with rich terminal stages and ogee cupolas

E.C.A.—C

12 HENRY VII'S CHAPEL, WESTMINSTER ABBEY
Built 1502–19, the exterior of this sumptuous chapel displays the late Perpendicular style in all of its
magnificence, with richly traceried bay windows of complex plan ranged between octagonal buttresses
which rise to form ogee-capped turrets. Behind these are paired flying buttresses, linked by traceried webs
and curving upwards to meet the lofty clerestory, which is finished with a tier of lacy arcading and a
perforated parapet between slender pinnacled buttresses

The Greater Churches: Interiors
Norman to Perpendicular Gothic

Left
1 WINCHESTER CATHEDRAL, HANTS
The transept. Begun *c* 1080, Bishop Walkelin's great cathedral was designed with a bay system modelled on that of St Etienne, Caen. Architecturally it was superior to its prototype, but more severe in its expression although this would originally have been relieved by colour decoration

Right
2 PETERBOROUGH CATHEDRAL, NORTHANTS
The St Etienne type of bay, used also at Ely and Norwich, found its most elegant and richly ornamented expression in the Late Norman presbytery of Peterborough, a great abbey church built between 1170 and 1193

Left
3 DURHAM CATHEDRAL
Begun *c* 1091 and completed in 1133, this finest of all Romanesque churches was the first to be covered throughout with ribbed stone vaulting. A solemn rhythm is set up by the use of great cylindrical piers to support the main arcade's arches in the double bays, and shafted compound piers to carry the high transverse arches dividing the vaulting compartments

4 GLOUCESTER CATHEDRAL

The Early Norman naves of Gloucester and Tewkesbury owe their extraordinary grandeur to the use of giant plain-shafted cylindrical piers in close succession, supporting boldly moulded arches. These lofty arcades are unique in Romanesque architecture, although the original inspiration may have come from Tournus in Burgundy. At Tewkesbury the triforium is indicated by small subdivided arches in the plain upper wall face, but at Gloucester it is well defined and richly ornamented, although small in relation to the main arcade

5 SOUTHWELL CATHEDRAL, NOTTS

Built c 1130, the Late Norman nave of this minster is unique in England for its three tiers of wide and relatively low arches, forming unbroken arcades and creating an effect similar to that of a Roman aqueduct

6 NORWICH CATHEDRAL
The splendid late Norman central tower is richly arcaded
outside and in. Each inside face of the open lantern has first a
tier of six open arches of two orders, then three pairs of blind
arches between two open circles, and above this stage are
three tall windows behind a wall passage screened by arches
rising from angle-shafts above slender columns

Below
7 DURHAM CATHEDRAL
The western Lady Chapel or Galilee is a late Norman work of
c 1170. The interior is divided into five aisles by arcades of
almost Saracenic elegance, their wide chevron-ornamented
arches resting on slender Purbeck columns, originally in
lateral pairs only, having water-leaf capitals and moulded
abaci

10 WELLS CATHEDRAL, SOMERSET

Early English Gothic matured rapidly at Wells. Affinities with Roche can be seen in the transepts of c 1185, but the interior elevation of the nave, begun c 1200, is quite original and fully assured in its effect. The main arcade and the triforium of closely-spaced lancets are unbroken by vaulting-shafts, resulting in a strong horizontal emphasis. This is in complete contrast to the contemporary French striving for verticality

Above
9 ROCHE ABBEY, YORKS

The bay design of this ruined Cistercian abbey church is a significant transitional work of c 1160–70 French Gothic influence is most apparent in the pointed arches and compound-shafted piers of the main arcade, and in the plain lancet recesses of the triforium, whereas the clerestory windows still have round arches. Neither triforium nor clerestory have wall passages

Left
8 WORKSOP PRIORY, NOTTS

The influence of Southwell is apparent in this transitional nave of c 1180, but here the unbroken arcade of round-headed arches is surmounted by a tribune where narrow acutely-pointed openings alternate with wide round arches

11 SALISBURY CATHEDRAL, WILTS

The lofty main arcade of this great interior is perfectly proportioned, but flattened arches of the same width are used, with unhappy effect, to frame the paired and subdivided arches of the low triforium. This defect apart, Salisbury is all that is characteristic and best in the developed Early English style. As at Wells, no vaulting-shafts descend below the triforium arches to divide the bays and break the horizontal emphasis created by the stringcourse above the arcade

12 LINCOLN CATHEDRAL, THE ANGEL CHOIR

This beautiful early Decorated retrochoir, begun 1256, shows Westminster's influence in its decoration but not in its proportions, which were scaled to accord with those of St Hugh's Choir, built c 1200. It should be noted that single screens of geometrical tracery were used to divide the tribune arches, whereas double tracery was introduced with exquisite effect in the clerestory. This reversed what was done at Westminster

Bottom left
13 SELBY ABBEY, YORKS

The late Decorated quire, completed c 1340, has the two-stage elevation typical of later Gothic interior elevations. The canopied figures in the main arcade's spandrels, the perforated parapet to the open walk below the clerestory windows, the beautiful curvilinear tracery in the great east window, and the tierceron vaulting of wood imitating stone, are all features of note in this lovely interior

Bottom right
14 BRISTOL CATHEDRAL

The Augustinian monastery's choir was rebuilt 1298–1330 as a hall-church having aisles as high as the wide central vessel. The mouldings of the lofty arcade's arches rise unbroken from base to apex, but there are carved capitals to the single engaged shafts supporting the central lierne vault, the first example of its type. Transverse arches in the aisles support miniature ribbed vaults covering each bay, and below the large windows of geometrical tracery are exquisite 'stellate' tomb recesses

15 GLOUCESTER CATHEDRAL

The first masterpiece of the new Perpendicular style was created in 1337–67, when Gloucester's choir was transformed into a Royal shrine of exceptional magnificence. A lofty clerestory was added and the rectilinear tracery of its windows was carried down to .veil the Early Norman arcades. An immense tripartite window, like a translucent tryptich, replaced the apse, and the interior was completed with a lierne vault of extreme complexity

Right
16 WINDSOR CASTLE, ST GEORGE'S CHAPEL

Built between 1478 and 1528, this cathedral-like chapel illustrates to perfection the late Perpendicular style as developed by the Royal masons. The elevations of the extremely wide central vessel are divided into narrow bays by slender vaulting shafts. Their vertical emphasis is repeated in the thin unbroken mouldings of the arcade's tall four-centred arches, the vertical panelling of the spandrels with their cresting of shield-bearing angels, and the rectilinear tracery of the lofty clerestory windows. Nowhere is the skill of the Royal masons more evident than in the marvellous low-pitched vaulting by William Vertue, with its spine of complex lierne stars flanked by fan-like arrangements of ribs

Round Naved Churches

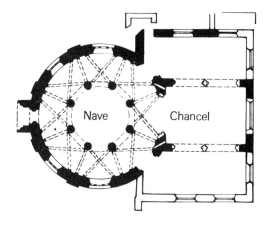

Nave · Chancel

1–3 (p. 42) CAMBRIDGE, CHURCH OF THE HOLY SEPULCHRE
The aisled round nave, built c 1200, is wholly Norman in style. The eight boldly moulded arches of the arcade rise from stout cylindrical piers with scalloped capitals. A similar but lower arcade of subdivided arches opens to the tribune, and there is a clerestory with one light to each bay. Between the tribune arches are wall shafts, rising from corbel heads to support the eight-part dome of wood, externally expressed by a restored conical roof. The aisle has stone-ribbed vaulting

4 LONDON, THE TEMPLE CHURCH OF ST MARY
The aisled round nave of 1160–85 is transitional in style although Gothic features predominate. The arcade has well-moulded pointed arches rising from compound piers of four Purbeck shafts, bound by annulets and finished with formal leaf capitals, but the false triforium is of Norman interlacing arcading, also with slender Purbeck shafts

41

Plans of Parish Churches

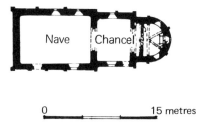

0   15 metres

1 KILPECK, HEREFORDS
St Mary and St David's Church. A small Norman
church of three-cell plan, the chancel apse-ended

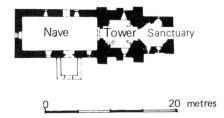

0   20 metres

2 STUDLAND, DORSET
St Nicholas's Church. A small Norman three-cell
church with a central choir-tower

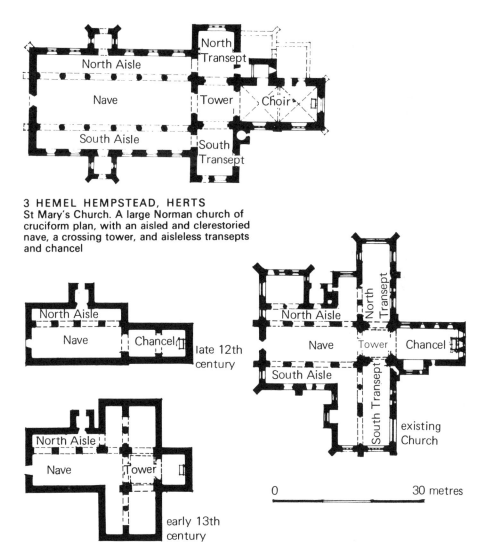

3 HEMEL HEMPSTEAD, HERTS
St Mary's Church. A large Norman church of
cruciform plan, with an aisled and clerestoried
nave, a crossing tower, and aisleless transepts
and chancel

0   30 metres

4 WITNEY, OXON
St Mary's Church. Three plans showing the
growth of a town church, from its small Norman
nucleus to its present spacious cruciform plan

Aisleless cruciform churches with crossing-towers

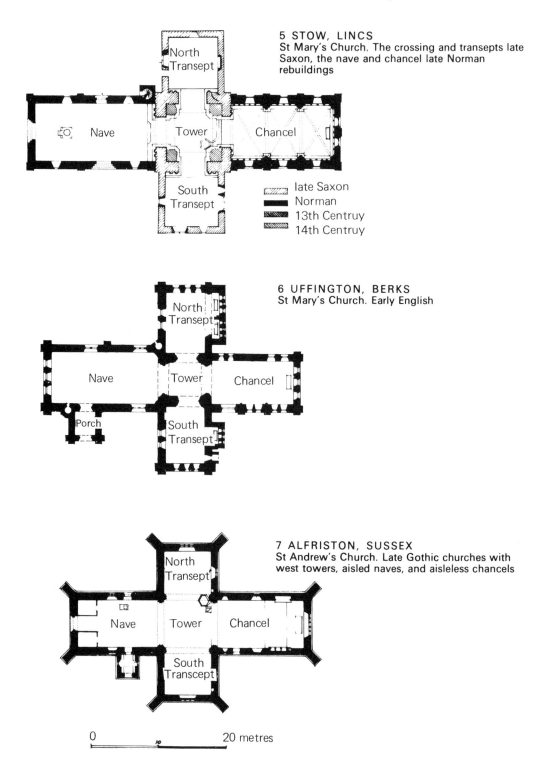

5 STOW, LINCS
St Mary's Church. The crossing and transepts late Saxon, the nave and chancel late Norman rebuildings

North Transept

Nave

Tower

Chancel

South Transept

late Saxon
Norman
13th Centruy
14th Centruy

6 UFFINGTON, BERKS
St Mary's Church. Early English

North Transept

Nave

Tower

Chancel

Porch

South Transept

7 ALFRISTON, SUSSEX
St Andrew's Church. Late Gothic churches with west towers, aisled naves, and aisleless chancels

North Transept

Nave

Tower

Chancel

South Transcept

0   10   20 metres

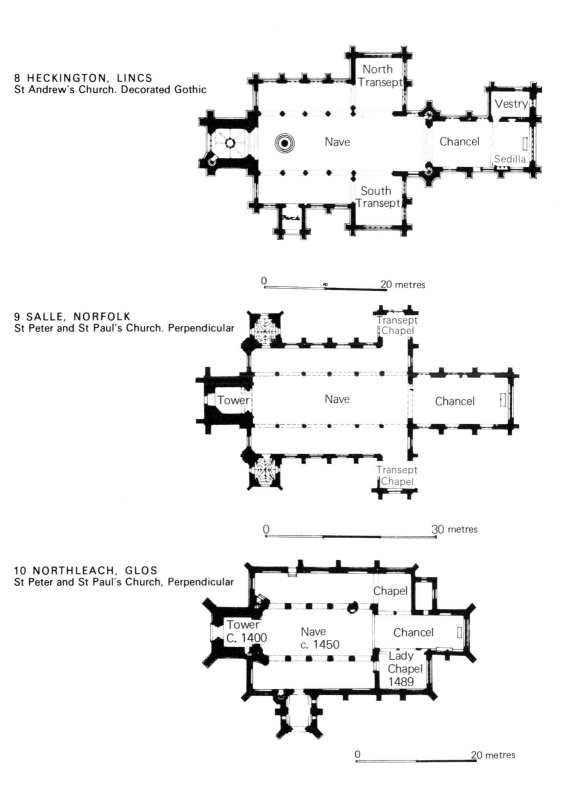

8 HECKINGTON, LINCS
St Andrew's Church. Decorated Gothic

North Transept

Nave

Chancel

Vestry

Sedilla

South Transept

0   10   20 metres

9 SALLE, NORFOLK
St Peter and St Paul's Church. Perpendicular

Transept Chapel

Tower

Nave

Chancel

Transept Chapel

0   30 metres

10 NORTHLEACH, GLOS
St Peter and St Paul's Church, Perpendicular

Chapel

Tower C. 1400

Nave c. 1450

Chancel

Lady Chapel 1489

0   20 metres

Large cruciform churches

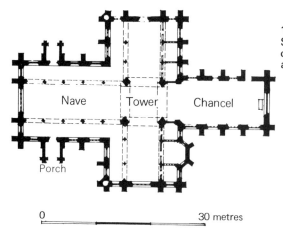

Nave   Tower   Chancel

Porch

0   30 metres

11 PATRINGTON, YORKS
St Patrick's Church. A splendid Decorated church
of cruciform plan, the nave and transepts with
aisles

Lady
Chapel

Transept

Nave   Choir

Transept

0   60 metres

12 BRISTOL
St Mary's Church, Redcliffe. An exceptionally
grand church of the Decorated and Perpendicular
periods, cruciform in plan with aisles to each arm
and an eastern Lady Chapel

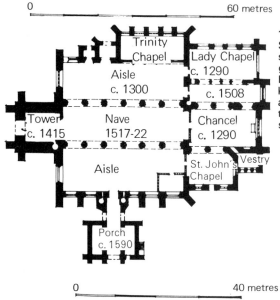

Trinity
Chapel   Lady Chapel
c. 1290
Aisle
c. 1300   c. 1508

Tower   Nave   Chancel
c. 1415   1517-22   c. 1290

Aisle   St. John's   Vestry
Chapel

Porch
c. 1590

0   40 metres

13 CIRENCESTER, GLOS
St John's Church. A parish church enlarged by
successive additions and rebuildings to its present
great size and splendour
Round Churches were generally built by the two
knightly orders founded to protect the Holy Land
and the Holy Sepulchre, the church from which
they take their form. Five churches of this type
survive in England

Parish Churches: Exteriors
Norman

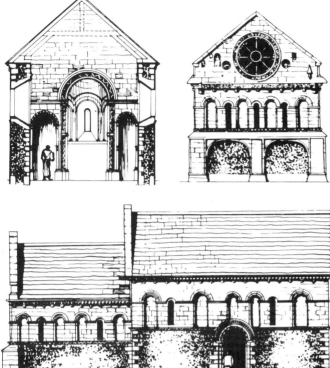

Left
1 BARFRESTON, KENT
This small church has a simple
two-cell plan, and its remarkably
lavish decoration of arcading and
carved ornament may be due to a
partial rebuilding of *c* 1180

Below
2 KILPECK, HEREFORDS
A three-cell church with an apse-
ended chancel (plan on p. 43).
Noteworthy external features are the
south doorway (detail on p. 66) and
the richly ornamented corbel-table,
supported by a remarkable series of
grotesque corbels extending between
shallow buttresses

Above
3 STEWKLEY, BUCKS
A three-cell church of *c* 1150, restored in 1862
by G.E.Street. The nave has a west door flanked
by blind arches, and a large south porch. The
choir is below the central tower, and the
square-ended chancel is rib-vaulted. Chevron
ornament enriches the doorways, the window
arches, and the interlacing arcading of the tower

4 IFFLEY, OXON
This church of *c* 1170 has a three-cell plan
similar to that of Stewkley. The well-composed
west front is remarkable for the wealth of chevron
and beakhead ornament lavished on the door and
windows

5 ST MARGARET AT CLIFFE, KENT
This large and splendid late Norman church has
an aisled nave with a clerestory of two-light
windows contained in a continuous arcade. The
aisleless and square-ended chancel is well lit by
tall single-light windows

6 UFFINGTON, BERKS

This little altered Early English church of cruciform plan is aisleless, but has shallow chapels projecting east from the transepts (plan on p. 44). Conspicuous features of the simply detailed exterior are the handsome two-storied south porch to the nave, the gabled east doorway to the south transept, and the octagonal central tower which rises from broaches and was originally surmounted by a spire

7 PATRING- TON, YORKS

A Decorated Gothic church of exceptional splendour, begun *c* 1325 to a cruciform plan having aisles to the nave and transepts (plan on p. 46). Noteworthy external features are the large windows of geometrical and curvilinear tracery, in bays between pinnacled buttresses, and the lovely central tower, its square shaft surmounted by a tall spire rising out of an arcaded octagonal corona

8 HECKING- TON, LINCS

This exquisite Decorated Gothic church, begun *c* 1345, has a tall spire-crowned west tower and a lofty clerestoried nave which extends east of the transept-chapels ending the aisles (plan on p. 45). Each transept- chapel of two bays, and the aisleless chancel of three bays, are lit by handsome windows of geometrical or curvilinear tracery

9 BOSTON, LINCS

Although this is one of England's largest and finest churches, and a noble example of Decorated Gothic, it is dwarfed by the immense Perpendicular west tower, which rises 272 feet to the rich cresting of its octagonal lantern

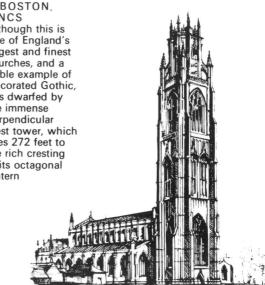

E.C.A.—D

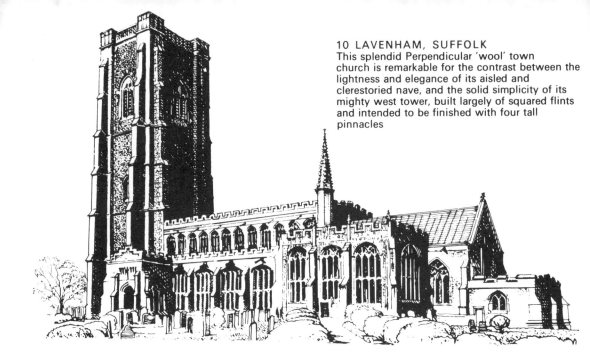

10 LAVENHAM, SUFFOLK
This splendid Perpendicular 'wool' town
church is remarkable for the contrast between the
lightness and elegance of its aisled and
clerestoried nave, and the solid simplicity of its
mighty west tower, built largely of squared flints
and intended to be finished with four tall
pinnacles

Left
11 SOUTHWOLD, SUFFOLK
Built *c* 1430, this great Perpendicular town
church is an outstanding example of East Anglian
flush flintwork, exhibited here in plain walling,
with stone chequers, and as panelling in
rectilinear stone tracery

Right
12 LONG MELFORD, SUFFOLK
The nine-bays long body of this splendid
Perpendicular church has a clerestory of
three-light windows extending unbroken below a
battlemented parapet, and tall aisle windows with
two tiers of three lights, arranged in pairs
between the buttresses. Here also there is a
superb display of elaborate flint flushwork

13 BRISTOL, ST MARY REDCLIFFE

With an aisled cruciform plan and a large eastern Lady Chapel, this is the most cathedral-like of all the great parish churches (plan on p. 46). Partly built in the late Decorated style of the early 1400s, it was completed in the sumptuous Perpendicular style which predominates externally. Here, as at Bath Abbey, the unusually narrow transept results in an oblong crossing

14 BRISTOL, ST MARY REDCLIFFE

This detail of the exterior shows the nave's south porch with its rich tabernacle-work, the aisle windows with their four-centred arches, the tall pinnacled buttresses supporting the flying buttresses, and the lofty clerestory where the windows have two-centred arches and the spandrels are panelled below a parapet of open trefoils framed in triangles

Left
15 CIRENCESTER, GLOS

The complex plan of this great 'wool' church resulted from a series of enlargements and rebuildings during times of prosperity (plan on p. 46). These works culminated with the lofty nave of 1516–30, and gave the church its predominantly rich late Perpendicular character. The magnificent and unique three-storied south porch was built *c* 1490 by Cirencester's abbot, to serve as his secular office

Parish Churches: Interiors
Norman

Above
1 STUDLAND, DORSET
The nave of this three-cell church opens to the tower-choir through an arch formed of two orders rising from angle-shafts with curiously carved capitals. The extrados of the arch is simply moulded with a roll or bowtell, and traces of original painted ornament survive on the intrados, which is unmoulded

Above
2 ELKSTONE, GLOS
Here also the tower arch has two orders, rising from shafts with scalloped capitals, but whereas the intrados is unmoulded, the extrados is highly enriched with chevrons and has a pelleted hoodmould rising from grotesque animal-heads. Both tower-choir and sanctuary are rib-vaulted in stone

3 COMPTON, SURREY
The late twelfth century nave has massive arcades with wide and simply moulded arches rising from stumpy cylindrical piers, their capitals either scalloped or carved with foliage. Beyond the earlier choir is the late twelfth century chancel, covered by a ribbed vault of stone and surmounted by a chapel or upper chancel, screened by a contemporary arcade of wood. This two-storied arrangement, now unique to Compton, was originally also to be found at Melbourne

4 ST MARGARET AT CLIFFE, KENT
This large and imposing church of *c* 1150 has a lofty nave with a plain clerestory above the fine arcades, their chevron-ornamented arches resting alternately on compound-shafted and cylindrical piers with scalloped capitals. The noble chancel arch opens to a deep aisleless choir, its east wall containing three tall windows below a small one of two lights

Right
5 STONE, KENT
Built *c* 1250, this early Decorated church has some affinities with Westminster Abbey, notably in the simple geometrical tracery of its windows, and the elegance of its nave arcades, their subtly-moulded arches resting on slender piers of clustered shafts, formed of stone and Purbeck marble, and finished with lovely stiff-leaf capitals

6 ABINGDON, BERKS
By a process of lateral enlargement, the width of this church is greater than its length. There are five aisles of similar width, linked by simple late Perpendicular arcades of low four-centred arches resting on slender octagonal shafted piers with cornice-profiled capitals

7 WEST WALTON, NORFOLK
The nave of this exquisite Early English church has two stages, both arcaded. The wide two-centred arches of the main arcade are rich moulded and rest on large circular abaci, each supported by the stiff-leaf capitals of four slenc Purbeck shafts and the stone columns to whicl they are linked by an annulet ring. The single lancet windows of the clerestory are placed in alternate bays of a delicate arcade, its simply-moulded arches resting on single shafts with plain capitals

8 CLEY-ON-SEA, NORFOLK

This grand but unfinished late Decorated church has a long nave of singular beauty. The widely-spaced arcades are simply treated, but centred over each octagonal pier is a richly carved corbel below a crocketted pinnacle, intended as a figure-tabernacle. Two strongly contrasted tracery patterns are used in the clerestory windows. Above each arch of the main arcade, the window is dominated by a large circle framing a cusped cinquefoil, whereas over each pier the window is simply divided into two cusp-headed lights below a small quatrefoil

9 SALLE, NORFOLK

Harmonious in style throughout; this glorious Perpendicular church has a clerestoried nave of six bays, with lofty arcades opening to wide aisles and transept-chapels. The aisleless chancel is three bays long and square ended. The nave's arch-braced timber roof is simply decorated with small angel-bosses covering the junctions of the moulded purlins and principal rafters. The short arch-braces rest on corbels which are, in fact, projections of the principal rafters supporting the aisle roofs

10 CHIPPING CAMPDEN, GLOS

The late Perpendicular nave of this noble 'wool' church has a simple and elegant bay design. The lofty arcade is composed of subtly moulded four-centred arches resting on tall concave-sided octagonal piers with cornice-profiled capitals. Above each arch the wall face is recessed to form a shallow arch with a two-centred head, framing a clerestory window divided and subdivided by rectilinear tracery to form four tall lights below three small foliated lights

Above
11 CIRENCESTER, GLOS

This magnificent late Perpendicular church, the largest in the county, is exceptional for its extremely lofty arcades, dividing the nave from the wide aisles. The tall piers, of slender shafts separated by hollows, rise from their richly modelled bases to carry the chamfered and moulded arches. These have hoodmoulds springing from shield-bearing angels. As at Campden and Northleach, the clerestory is returned above the chancel arch, here with a wide window of seven lights

12 GREAT BARDFIELD, ESSEX

The lofty, clerestoried nave of this late Decorated church is separated from the chancel by an arch containing a rood-screen of rich curvilinear stone tracery, resembling an unglazed window with three tall lights

Interior Elevations
Anglo-Norman (Romanesque)

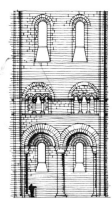

1 JUMIEGES, NORMANDY
Abbey Church of Notre Dame (1036–66). This noble and austere double-bay scheme probably inspired the design of Edward the Confessor's Westminster Abbey, built c 1050–65, and its influence can be seen in Durham Cathedral

2 DURHAM CATHEDRAL (c 1093–1133)
A double-bay in the eastern arm, and a half cross section showing the rib-vaulted aisle and a transverse arch in the tribune, serving to buttress the high ribbed vaulting of the central vessel. In the western arm, built later, these arches were replaced by half arches, prototypes of the Gothic flying buttresses

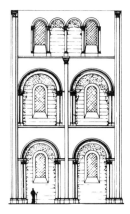

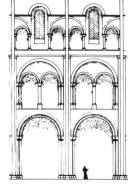

3 CAEN, NORMANDY
Abbey Church of St Etienne (begun c 1068). The paired bays of the nave have aisle and tribune arcades of equal architectural importance. The nave was originally finished with a flat wooden ceiling above the lofty clerestory, then a 'thick wall' containing a passage having open arcades of four small arches centred over each pair of bays. St Etienne was the prototype most commonly adopted in the great Anglo-Norman churches

4 WINCHESTER CATHEDRAL, HANTS (c 1079)
The Perpendicular casing transformed the nave of this immense cathedral, one of the earliest Anglo-Norman churches. Extremely austere in expression, the bay design improves on its prototype, St Etienne, in its subdivided tribune arches and the trios of stepped arches screening the clerestory passage. The bay design survives unaltered in the transepts

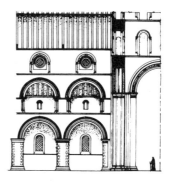

5 PETERBOROUGH CATHEDRAL, NORTHANTS (c 1180)

The presbytery's elevation of single bays is the most sophisticated and richly ornamented of all the 'St Etienne' bays

6 SOUTHWELL CATHEDRAL, NOTTS (c 1130)

The nave elevation has three arcaded stages, with no vertical demarcation of the bays. The aisle and tribune arcades are of equal architectural importance, and the round windows of the clerestory are recessed in a series of smaller arches. This aqueduct-like design was possibly inspired by Tournai Cathedral's nave, built c 1100, and its influence can be seen at Worksop Priory

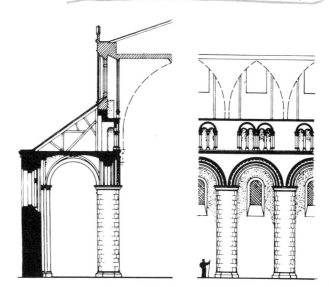

8 OXFORD CATHEDRAL (c 1170)

The Late Norman bay design is a sophisticated and refined version of the scheme used in the presbytery of Gloucester, but having a triforium arcade of three small arches in the recessed tympanum above the arch opening to the aisle

7 GLOUCESTER CATHEDRAL (c 1100)

The nave elevation is the latest and most richly decorated example of a design peculiar to a small group of important West Country Benedictine churches, all employing a very lofty and closely spaced arcade of richly moulded arches rising from giant plain-shafted cylindrical piers. Although the giant arcade was repeated in the presbytery, each arch there was divided horizontally by a recessed arch to form openings to the ambulatory and tribune

Transitional and Early English Gothic

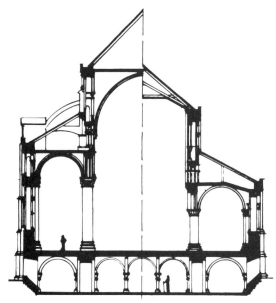

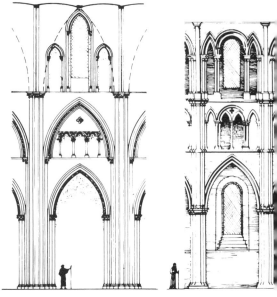

Below

9 CANTERBURY CATHEDRAL, KENT (*c* 1180)

Longitudinal section through the Trinity Chapel and Corona, a work of French Gothic inspiration, probably begun by William of Sens and completed by William the Englishman. The lofty ambulatory arcade shows a mixed use of plain cylindrical and compound-shafted piers, with 'Corinthian' capitals. Pointed and round arches are used in the triforium, and the clerestory lancets are set in a plain wall behind delicate screens of pointed arcading. The lavish use of Purbeck marble for piers, shafts, abaci and stringcourses, derived from Flanders and continued to be an important decorative feature in many Early English churches.

Top left

10 GLASTONBURY ABBEY, SOMERSET (*c* 1190)

This great church, now in ruins, was built about the same time as Wells Cathedral, nearby, but the two buildings had little in common. Glastonbury's bay design was an Early English Gothic version of the Late Norman scheme used at Oxford

Top right

11 RIPON CATHEDRAL, YORKS (*c* 1190)

A Transitional bay in the choir. The pointed arch of the main arcade reveals a round-headed window in the ambulatory, while narrow sharply-pointed arches flank the round-headed middle arches of the triforium and clerestory which frame, respectively, a pair of pointed arches and a round-headed window

Above

12 WELLS CATHEDRAL, SOMERSET (*c* 1200)

Part elevation of the nave, and half transverse section. This beautiful Early English bay design has an unbroken arcade of richly-moulded pointed arches rising from compound-shafted piers with stiff-leaf capitals, a triforium composed of narrow lancet openings, each recessed within a taller and boldly-moulded lancet, and a clerestory of large lancets, each set in the tympanum formed by the simple ribbed vaulting. This rises from short shafts above corbels in the triforium, and is partially supported by flying buttresses concealed by the aisle roofs

Above right

13 SALISBURY CATHEDRAL, WILTS (*c* 1220)

The bay design used throughout this most uniform of Early English cathedrals is of the usual three stages. The main arcade is lofty and well proportioned, the arch spandrels unbroken as at Wells. The richly modelled triforium is rather squat, with a wide depressed arch framing two subdivided arches, while the clerestory has three lancets behind a screen, its arches stepped to conform with the ribbed vaulting. The grey Chilmark stone is elaborately dressed with Purbeck marble

14 BOXGROVE PRIORY, SUSSEX (*c* 1220).

This unusual scheme was used earlier at Portsmouth Cathedral. The pointed arches of the aisle arcade are paired within large round arches, each surmounted by a clerestory with one tall lancet behind a screen of three arches, stepped to conform with the ribbed vaulting

Late Early English and Decorated Gothic

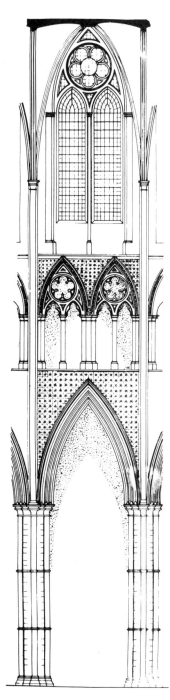

Left
15 WESTMINSTER ABBEY, LONDON (begun 1244)
Built by a master mason (probably Henry of Reyns) well acquainted with French High Gothic cathedrals such as Reims and Amiens. The bay design of the presbytery is remarkable for its narrow width, some 17 feet, related to its great height of 90 feet. Above the lofty main arcade is a richly decorated tribune, its two subdivided arches reproducing on a small scale the geometrical bar tracery of the tall clerestory window. The considerable use of Purbeck marble, and the retention of a deep triforium gallery, are typically English features in a French inspired design. The transverse section, taken through the nave, shows the elaborate system of flying buttresses used to support the high ribbed vaulting

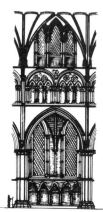

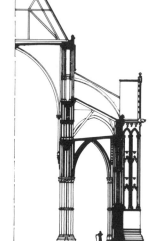

16 LINCOLN CATHEDRAL
Westminster's influence is obvious in the rich decoration of Lincoln's Angel Choir, built 1256—80, but the wide and relatively low proportions of the bay design were dictated by the need to conform with the earlier St Hugh's Choir, begun *c* 1200, and the nave of *c* 1225 where the bays are even wider. The beautiful double tracery of Geometrical pattern, and the lavish use of Purbeck marble, are typical of the first phase of Decorated Gothic

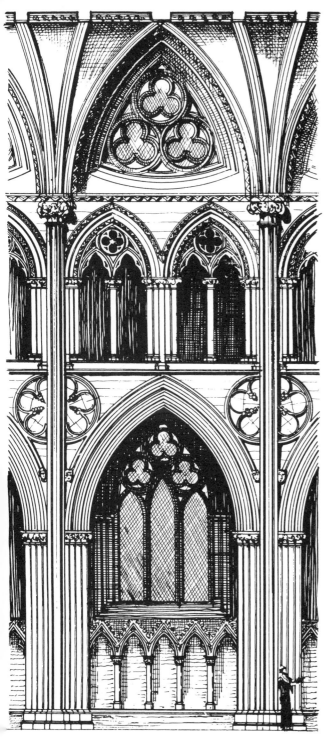

17 LICHFIELD CATHEDRAL, STAFFS (1250–80)
A richly ornamented and ingeniously designed bay, the nave's lack of height overcome by using a clerestory composed of convex-sided triangular windows, each containing three foliated circles. Similar windows were used to light the tribune gallery at Westminster, and were probably derived from those in the lower Sainte Chapelle in Paris

Above
18 YORK MINSTER
The bay design of the nave, built 1291–1324, shows the growing tendency to use only two lofty stages, the main arcade being surmounted by a clerestory with windows of Geometrical tracery, each divided into five lights by mullions which are carried down to flank the small gabled openings of the triforium passage

63

Perpendicular Gothic

Below
19 CANTERBURY CATHEDRAL, KENT
The nave was rebuilt *c* 1378–1405 on the Norman foundations.
Although somewhat conventional when compared with other
Perpendicular works, Henry Yevele's nave is a supremely elegant and
accomplished design. The spatial effect is that of a hall church, the
aisles being lit by immense windows of rectilinear tracery, whereas the
nave has only a small clerestory above the lofty arcades

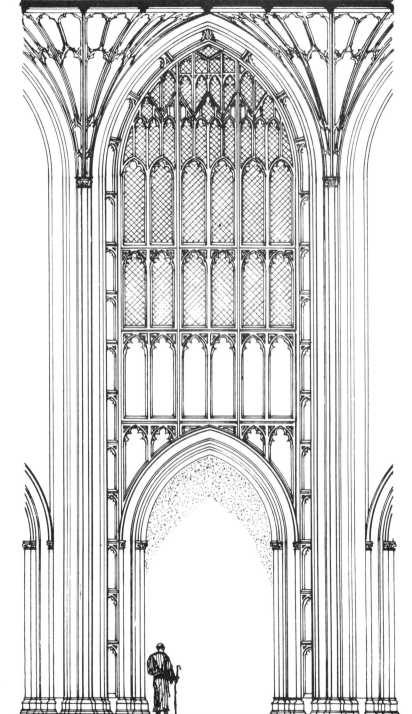

20 SHERBORNE ABBEY, DORSET
The presbytery, rebuilt *c* 1430–50, shows the ultimate development of English Gothic bay design. Here each bay of the ambulatory arcade and each clerestory window are recessed in a giant arch, its splayed reveal decorated with cusped panels. The rectilinear tracery of the window is carried down to form panelling over the spandrels of the arcade's arches. Groups of slender shafts rise between the giant arches to provide the springing for the fully developed fan vaulting

E.C.A.—E

Doorways and Porches
Norman

1 KILPECK, HEREFORDS
St Mary and St David's Church. The remarkable south doorway of this famous Norman church is enriched with the conventional chevron and beakhead ornaments, and with elaborate carving such as the Tree of Life in the semicircular tympanum, the two superimposed warriors of the left column-shaft, and the intertwining dragons of the jambs, these last showing strong Scandinavian influence

3 BRISTOL, ST MARY REDCLIFFE'S CHURCH

The outer north porch is a sumptuous structure of hexagonal plan with a parvise above. It was built *c* 1320 as an ante-chapel to Our Lady's shrine. The main doorway is a fantastic arch of three orders, scalloped and decorated like the jambs with rich formal foliage ornament, the head of the arch being intricately formed with trilobed cusps. While suggesting the luxurious elaboration of Indian art, the work has kinship with the late Gothic of Portugal

Below
4 LICHFIELD CATHEDRAL, STAFFS

Here the nave is entered through a shallow porch, its framing arch integrated with the arcaded first stage of the west front. The arch of two highly enriched orders is cusped inside and rises from shafted jambs decorated, like the trumeau between the inner doors, with canopied figures

2 WELLS CATHEDRAL, SOMERSET

The nave's west portal is a minor feature of the great sculptural screen forming the west front. An arch of three moulded orders frames the doorway, where two pointed openings are divided by a single shaft below a large quatrefoil

5 NORTHLEACH, GLOS

St Peter and St Paul's Church. The nave of this great Perpendicular church is entered through a large south porch of two stories. The front is divided by a vertical sequence of niched and canopied figures rising above the ogee hoodmould of the entrance arch. Gabled niches also ornament the diagonal buttresses and the blind lights of the parvise windows

Windows
Norman

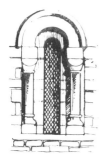

Left

1 SANDFORD, OXON
St Martin's Church. A single-light window of
c 1120, recessed in an unmoulded arch rising
from angle-shafts with cushion capitals

2 DEVIZES, WILTS
St John's Church. A window of *c* 1160, its one
large light handsomely framed by an arch,
enriched with chevron and a pelletted
hoodmould, rising from slender angle-shafts with
scalloped capitals

Gothic

3 STONE, KENT
St Mary's Church. This late Early English window
has the glass set in plate tracery forming two
lancets below a quatrefoil, and it is recessed
behind a screen of bar tracery with slender
Purbeck shafts supporting trefoiled arches in a
tympanum, pierced with a large quatrefoil flanked
by small circles

Left

4 GRANTHAM, LINCS
St Wulfram's Church. The large west window of the north aisle is divided by Decorated tracery of
geometrical form. There are two sub-arches, each divided into three tall lights below three circles, and
above is a large circle framing seven small circles, none of them cusped

5 LEOMINSTER, HEREFORDS
St Peter and St Paul's Church. The Decorated south aisle is lit by a series of large windows of late
geometrical tracery. Each window is divided into two sub-arches of two cusp-headed lights below pointed
cinquefoils, and above the sub-arches is a large circle divided by radial bars to form pointed trefoils and
quatrefoils alternately. The shafts and tracery are noteworthy for their wealth of ballflower ornament

6 WELLS CATHEDRAL, SOMERSET

The octagonal chapter house has in each face a lovely window of late geometrical tracery, with two sub-arches each divided into two cusp-headed lights below elongated trefoils. The head of each sub-arch contains a small circle, decorated like the large circle in the main arch with ogee cusping

8 NANTWICH, CHESHIRE

St Mary's Church. The great east window is a typical example of Perpendicular rectilinear tracery, with two sub-arches of three lights flanking the middle light. The upper parts of all seven lights are divided by super-mullions

7 SLEAFORD, LINCS

St Denys's Church. This late Decorated window is divided by curvilinear or flamboyant tracery, forming two sub-arches of two lights, and a head composed largely of mouchettes

Circular or Rose Windows

Above
9 BARFRESTON, KENT
St Nicholas's Church. In the chancel's east wall is
a late Norman wheel window, the 'spokes'
formed of shafts with grotesque mask capitals.
The surround of the window is enriched with
grotesque carvings of foliage and monsters

Above
10 LINCOLN CATHEDRAL
The north transept's rose window contains Early
English plate tracery, the design composed of a
large subdivided quatrefoil surrounded by small
circles

11 LINCOLN CATHEDRAL
The exquisite late Decorated rose window of the
south transept contains curvilinear tracery, with a
pattern of mouchettes framed by two vesicas and
the triangular spaces between them

12 BOYTON, WILTS
St Cosmas and St Damian's Church. The east
window of the south chapel is a circle, divided by
geometrical tracery into three convex-sided
triangles containing quatre-foiled circles. The
interspaces contain small trefoiled circles

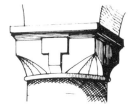

1 LONDON, TOWER OF LONDON, KEEP
St John's Chapel. The early Norman piers have square stepped bases, plain round shafts, and square capitals of two types, one having two scallops on each face, the other with T-crosses between concave leaf-moulded angles

2 CHRIST-CHURCH PRIORY, HANTS
The compound-shafted piers of the nave's tribune arcades have Corinthianesque capitals

Below
4 NORTHAMPTON, ST PETER'S CHURCH
The nave arcades, built c 1150, have round piers with varied capitals. This one suggests some Byzantine influence, with its woven band of reeding above the inverted palmettes, and its rich abacus of inter-related leaves

5 WALSOKEN, NORFOLK
All Souls Church. The late Norman chancel arch is pointed and its three orders are enriched with chevrons and a nailhead hoodmould. The angle-shafts have annulet-rings and scalloped capitals

3 CANTERBURY CATHEDRAL
The late Norman crypt has a marvellous series of richly carved capitals, ranking high among the works of English Romanesque sculpture. Their basically cushion form is dissolved by the profusion of motifs, generally grotesque human forms fighting strange monsters

Above
6 COMPTON BASSET, WILTS
St Swithun's Church. The arches of the nave's late twelfth century arcades rest on round piers with trumpet-scalloped capitals and moulded square abaci

7 WHAPLODE, LINCS
St Mary's Church. The early twelfth century nave arcades have moulded arches resting on square abaci above the scalloped capitals of piers which are alternately round and square, although the latter are moulded to appear as a group of eight shafts

8 LINCOLN CATHEDRAL

The nave's west doorway is a superb late Norman work, the arch of five orders rising from responds and angle-shafts highly enriched with vigorous carving, beakheads clasping the respond-shafts, grotesque animals and human figures ornamenting the other shafts, and formalized foliage ornament on the scalloped capitals

Gothic

Below

9 LINCOLN CATHEDRAL

In the Angel Choir of 1256–80, the arcade's compound piers are formed with an octagonal core of stone having a Purbeck shaft slightly recessed in each diagonal face. The exquisite stiff-leaf capitals are surmounted by a Purbeck marble abacus

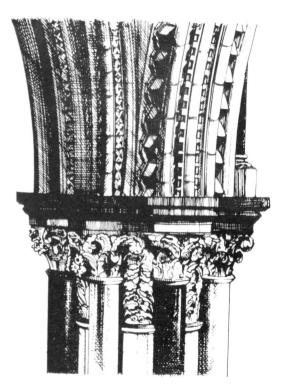

10–13 CANTERBURY CATHEDRAL, KENT

10 11 The arcades of the choir, begun 1175, have plain-shafted columns with Corinthianesque capitals of stone and Purbeck marble abaci.
12   The four compound piers of the east transept crossing have an octagonal stone core surrounded by eight slender shafts of Purbeck marble, all with foliage capitals of Corinthianesque type. Chevrons, billets and nailheads ornament the orders of the arches.
13   The arcades of the Trinity Chapel's apse have arches of two moulded orders rising from laterally paired columns of Purbeck marble, with rich Corinthianesque capitals of stone and Purbeck abaci

14–15 WELLS CATHEDRAL, SOMERSET
These finely carved stiff-leaf capitals are enlivened with figure-subjects relating to the mundane life

Left
16 LICHFIELD CATHEDRAL, STAFFS
The chapter house of *c* 1250, an elongated octagon in plan, has a stone-ribbed vault resting centrally on a compound-shafted pier, with richly carved foliage capitals to the shafts, and a large circular abacus

17–19 SOUTHWELL CATHEDRAL, NOTTS
The beautiful early Decorated chapter house is noteworthy for its wealth of finely carved capitals, with their realistic use of natural foliage forms. (17) Maple. (18) Hawthorn, with a 'Green Man'. (19) Hawthorn and oak capitals, and hop-vine on the arch

20 PATRINGTON, YORKS
St Patrick's Church. This magnificent Decorated church has arcades with richly moulded arches resting on diagonally-placed compound-shafted piers finished with freely carved foliage capitals

21–22 HAMPTON POYLE AND WOODSTOCK, OXON
A regional feature was the use, in the fourteen and fifteenth centuries, of capitals featuring or wholly composed of human features, such as male and female heads peering out of foliage a Woodstock, and the grotesque armour-clad soldiers at Hampton Poyle

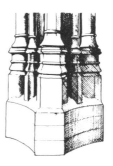

23–25 LONDON, WESTMINSTER ABBEY
The main arcades, although at first sight uniform, vary with the three main building periods.
(23) Those in the presbytery date from c 1245 and have circular piers with four engaged Purbeck marble shafts. (24) Those in the east bays of the nave, built c 1260, have eight shafts although only four are of Purbeck marble. (25) In the west part of the nave, built c 1380 by Henry Yevele, the piers also have eight engaged shafts but they rise from more elaborately moulded bases and have more prominent annulet-rings

27 BLOXHAM, OXON
Our Lady's Church. The compound-shafted piers have richly-moulded baluster bases and are placed diagonally on plain concave-sided plinths

26 ELY CATHEDRAL, CAMBS
In the sumptuously ornamented retrochoir, built 1234–52, the arcade piers are composed of a central column and eight detached shafts, all of Purbeck marble, their moulded bases resting on a stepped octagonal plinth ornamented with carved masks and foliage

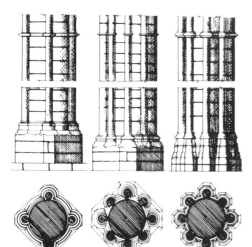

Stone Vaulting

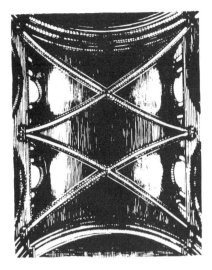

Right
2 BEVERLEY
MINSTER, YORKS
The single bays of the
Early English choir, built
c 1230, are covered with
simple quadripartite
vaulting, more elegant in
style but basically
similar to the Norman
vaulting at Durham

Above
1 DURHAM CATHEDRAL
Norman quadripartite vaulting in the nave,
completed c 1133. Massive slightly-pointed
arches separate the single and double bays.
Diagonal ribs intersect to divide each double bay
into seven cells and each single bay into four.
The transverse arches and ribs are boldly moulded
and enriched with chevron ornament

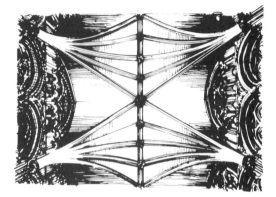

Above
3 LINCOLN CATHEDRAL
The Angel Choir of c 1256–80. In this vaulting
extra ribs, tiercerons, are introduced to divide the
cells of the longitudinal vault. The ridge-rib is
broken by large bosses where the diagonal ribs
intersect it, and smaller bosses form stops for the
transverse ribs and tiercerons

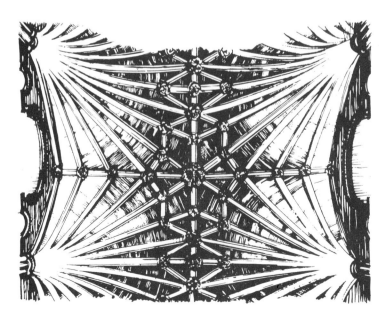

Left
4 NORWICH CATHEDRAL
The elaborate late fifteenth
century vaulting of the
presbytery has a fan-like
arrangement of ribs expanding
from each group of wall shafts.
These ribs stop against bosses
breaking the longitudinal and
transverse ridge-ribs, and they
are linked by short ribs, liernes,
to form a series of stellar
patterns and allow more carved
bosses to be used

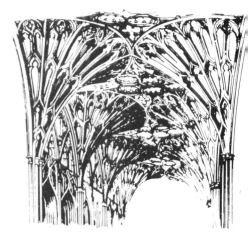

Right
6 GLOUCESTER CATHEDRAL
The cloisters of *c* 1410. Beautiful and perfectly formed fan vaulting covers the square bays of the Perpendicular cloister walk. Here, in the first important example of this form of vaulting, no transverse ribs divide the bays and break the sweep of the semi-conoid fans

Above
5 ELY CATHEDRAL, CAMBS
The Octagon of *c* 1330. Eight segments of wooden vaulting, elaborated with pseudo-tiercerons, effect the transition from the walls of the Octagon to its tall central lantern, a smaller octagon turned so that each of its angles rises from the crown of the vault below

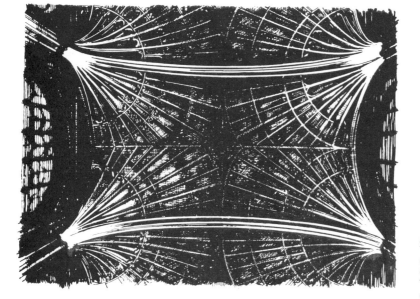

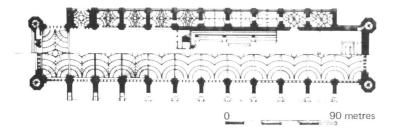

0   90 metres

Left
7 KING'S COLLEGE CHAPEL, CAMBRIDGE
The chapel was originally intended by its designer, Reginald of Ely, to have an elaborate lierne vault, but it was finished by John Wastell, around 1580, with a superb fan vault where the semi-conoids are divided by transverse ribs and converge on concave-sided lozenge panels containing carved bosses

Left
8 OXFORD CATHEDRAL
The choir. Probably designed by William
Orchard and constructed *c* 1478–1503, the
late Perpendicular vaulting of the Norman
choir has on each side a series of panelled
segmental arches, framing the clerestory
and resting on transverse arches dividing
the bays. These arches are then concealed
by semi-conoids having ribs rising,
apparently, from lantern bosses and
expanding to interlace and form stellar
patterns

Below
9 WESTMINSTER ABBEY
Henry VII's Chapel. This astonishing vault,
a masterpiece of late Perpendicular
masonry, was designed by William Vertue
and constructed *c* 1519. Although its
construction is basically similar to that of
the Oxford vault, it is far more elaborate,
with large pendant conoids in front of the
semi-conoids between the clerestory
windows, and small pendant conoids
placed in the middle of the bays

Perpendicular Gothic Timber Roofs

1 MARCH, CAMBS
St Wendreda's Church. This magnificent double-hammerbeam roof is richly decorated with carved ornament and has a host of winged angels, at the ends of the hammerbeams, on each tiebeam, and below the wallposts where they support canopied figures

2 CAWSTON, NORFOLK
St Agnes's Church. The nave roof, 48 feet wide, is steeply pitched and supported by single hammerbeam trusses alternating with simple arch-braced trusses. On the hammerbeams, which are carved and crested like the coved wallplates, stand tall angels with raised wings. Smaller angels decorate the wallplates

3 MILDENHALL, SUFFOLK
St Mary's Church. The low-pitched roof of the nave rests on arch-braced tiebeams, decorated with small angels, alternating with single hammerbeam trusses, decorated with large horizontal angels. The spandrels and tympana of the tiebeam trusses contain delicate arcaded tracery

4 NEEDHAM MARKET, SUFFOLK
St John's Church. The wide aisleless nave has an astonishing timber roof, formed with arch-braced hammerbeams supporting tall posts, linked laterally and transversely by cambered tiebeams. Just below the low-pitched ceiling is a clerestory of wood tracery

5 ELY CATHEDRAL, CAMBS

The transepts have fine hammerbeam roofs of fifteenth century date, the arch-braces below the hammerbeams rising from angel corbels and dying into the large angels decorating the hammerbeams

Below

6 SHEPTON MALLET, SOMERSET

St Peter and St Paul's Church. The wagon ceiling is as typical of the West Country as the hammerbeam type is of East Anglia. This wonderful Perpendicular example has 350 square panels, all finely carved with different Flamboyant designs and framed by moulded ribs, their mitred junctions hidden by exquisite foliage bosses

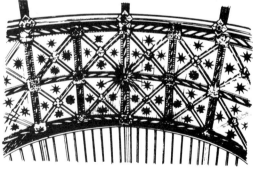

7 HENNOCK, DEVON

St Mary's Church. This wagon ceiling is of simple design except for the carved and painted celure above the roodscreen

Towers and Spires
Norman

Above
1 TEWKESBURY ABBEY, GLOS
The plain base of this splendid crossing-tower contains windows lighting the crossing. The upper part, with wide clasping buttresses, is divided by a tier of blind interlacing arcading into two low stages, also arcaded. The lower stage has three louvred arches in each face, whereas the upper has two sub-divided belfry windows

3 CASTOR, NORTHANTS
St Kyneburgha's Church. The late Norman crossing-tower is divided by rich corbel-tables into two arcaded stages without angle-buttresses. Each face of the lower stage has a large two-light window flanked by subdivided blind arches, whereas the upper stage is uniformly arcaded with five subdivided arches, the middle three open to serve as belfry windows

Above
2 NORWICH CATHEDRAL, NORFOLK
The finest and tallest of late Norman crossing-towers has a tall shaft elaborately patterned with arcading of various heights and forms, extending between reeded angle-turrets. Above the tall arcaded stage containing the lantern windows is a zone of vertical panels framing two tiers of circles

Left
4 LITTLE SAXHAM, SUFFOLK
St Nicholas's Church. A perfect Norman round tower, its plain flintwork shaft finished with a belfry stage where four subdivided open arches are linked by pairs of blind arches

Right
5 WEST WALTON, NORFOLK
St Mary's Church. This lovely Early English church has a detached campanile, standing well south of the nave. Massively built and strengthened with octagonal angle-turrets, it is decorated with delicate arcading, extending round the angle-turrets. Each face is similar in having a low stage with an arch to the open porch, a tall middle stage with three narrow arches, deeply recessed, and a lofty top stage with a large subdivided belfry window

6 BYTHORN, HUNTS
St Lawrence's Church. The simple
Decorated tower of three stages is
surmounted by a broach spire having three
tiers of dormers, or lucarnes

7 RAUNDS, NORTHANTS
St Mary's Church. The notable west steeple
consists of an Early English tower of four
well-proportioned stages, the west face of
the third curiously treated with a window
and four quatrefoil lights disposed within a
W-formed moulding. The handsome broach
spire rises from a corbel-table and has three
tiers of gabled lucarnes

8 EXTON, RUTLAND
St Peter and St Paul's Church. The
handsome early Decorated tower has a
shaft of three stages, strongly buttressed
and surmounted by four angle-turrets and
an octagonal lantern with a stone spire

9 GRANTHAM, LINCS
St Wulfram's Church. This magnificent
steeple has a lofty tower, Early English in its
lower stages and Decorated above. The tall
octagonal spire rises from broaches behind
octagonal pinnacles, the larger south-west
one crowning the stair-turret
Far Right
10 LOUTH, LINCS
St James's Church. This, the most
beautiful of all Perpendicular steeples, has a
lofty tower of three stages, handsomely
buttressed and surmounted by a slender
crocketted spire of octagonal plan, partly
supported by traceried flyers springing
diagonally behind the tall corner pinnacles

E.C.A.—F

11 GLOUCESTER CATHEDRAL

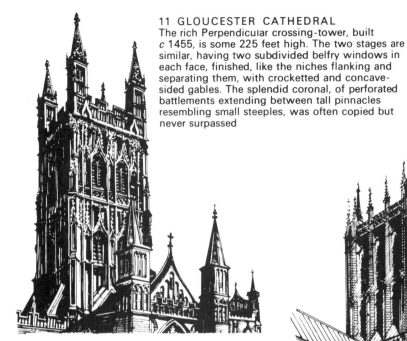

The rich Perpendicular crossing-tower, built
c 1455, is some 225 feet high. The two stages are
similar, having two subdivided belfry windows in
each face, finished, like the niches flanking and
separating them, with crocketted and concave-
sided gables. The splendid coronal, of perforated
battlements extending between tall pinnacles
resembling small steeples, was often copied but
never surpassed

12 WELLS CATHEDRAL, SOMERSET

As originally built in c 1321, the crossing-tower
had three tall lancet openings in each face. With
the late Perpendicular recasing of c 1440, the
upper parts of these lancets were transformed
into Somerset-traceried belfry openings, set in tall
square-headed recesses with arcaded aprons

Left
13 CANTERBURY CATHEDRAL, KENT

The tall shaft of John Wastell's beautiful
crossing-tower, built c 1496, rises some 250 feet.
Between boldly modelled octagonal turrets, each
face has two lofty stages divided by a slender
central buttress. The tall two-light windows of the
lantern stage have crocketted gables of ogee
form, whereas the generally similar belfry
windows have traceried spandrels. Perforated
battlements extend between the crowning
turrets, which are elaborated with gablets and
pinnacles

Below

14 WELLS, SOMERSET
St Cuthbert's Church. The noble Perpendicular west tower has a very tall belfry stage, its design clearly derived from the cathedral's west towers although it is more handsomely finished with panelled battlements between the tall corner pinnacles

15 TAUNTON, SOMERSET
St Mary Magdalene's Church. This magnificent Perpendicular tower is 163 feet high, rising in four well-defined stages. The upper three have, in each face, a pair of rich Somerset-traceried windows with ogee hoodmoulds. The coronal of perforated stonework, with its stepped battlements and square pinnacled turrets, clearly derives from Gloucester

16 HUISH EPISCOPI, SOMERSET
St Mary's Church. In a region famed for its beautiful towers, this one is outstanding. The three perfectly proportioned and differently fenestrated stages are surmounted by a handsome coronal of perforated battlements extending between richly crocketted pinnacles

17 CHIPPING CAMPDEN, GLOS

St James's Church. This splendid Perpendicular 'wool' church has an unusually fine west tower, simply decorated but most skilfully designed. Its three main stages are divided by moulded stringcourses which combine with the three slender buttresses on each face to form a grid-like frame for the subdivided windows in the upper two stages. The ogee hoodmoulds of the windows are echoed by the ogee arches with pinnacles, rising from the buttresses against the battlemented parapet

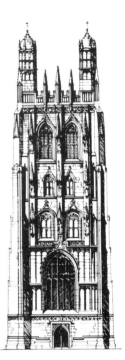

18 WREXHAM, DENBIGH

St Giles's Church, built c 1460, has a splendid west tower which was completed c 1520. Rising to a height of 135 feet, this splendid Perpendicular composition is worthy to rank with the masterpieces of the West Country masons. Its closest affinities are with the detached campanile of Evesham Abbey, built about the same time

Right
19 NEWCASTLE, NORTHUMBERLAND

St Nicholas's Cathedral. The Perpendicular west tower of this large cruciform church is remarkable for its open corona, formed by four flyers, or half-arches, springing behind pinnacled angle-turrets and rising diagonally to meet and support a small square lantern, crowned by a slender pinnacle

Left
20 INGATESTONE, ESSEX

This sturdy late Gothic tower is simply designed and finely built of red brick

Details of Mouldings and Decorations
Norman Ornamented Mouldings

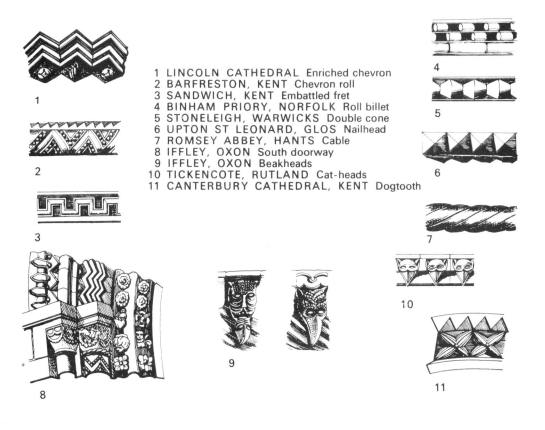

1 LINCOLN CATHEDRAL Enriched chevron
2 BARFRESTON, KENT Chevron roll
3 SANDWICH, KENT Embattled fret
4 BINHAM PRIORY, NORFOLK Roll billet
5 STONELEIGH, WARWICKS Double cone
6 UPTON ST LEONARD, GLOS Nailhead
7 ROMSEY ABBEY, HANTS Cable
8 IFFLEY, OXON South doorway
9 IFFLEY, OXON Beakheads
10 TICKENCOTE, RUTLAND Cat-heads
11 CANTERBURY CATHEDRAL, KENT Dogtooth

Norman Sculptural Decoration

1 TICKENCOTE, RUTLAND Vaulting-boss
2 KILPECK, HEREFORDS South doorway

3 STRETTON SUGWASH, HEREFORDS Doorway tympanum

Gothic Mouldings

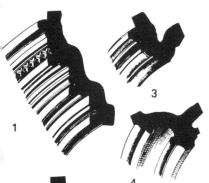

Arch mouldings

1 GREAT HASELEY, OXON West door arch (Early English, *c* 1220)
2 GREAT HASELEY, OXON North aisle door arch (Decorated, *c,* 1350)
3 KIDLINGTON, OXON Door arch (Decorated, *c* 1350)
4 GREAT HASELEY, OXON North aisle arcade (Perpendicular, *c* 1430)

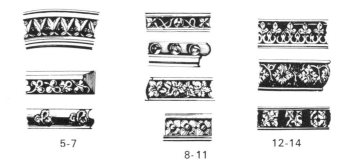

5-7   8-11   12-14

Ornamented mouldings

Early English
5 BINHAM PRIORY, NORFOLK Scrolled dogtooth, *c* 1280
6 WARMINGTON, NORTHANTS Trilobe foliage, *c* 1250
7 WINCHESTER CATHEDRAL, HANTS Trilobe foliage, *c* 1260

Decorated

8 BLOXHAM, OXON Ballflower and dogtooth, *c* 1280
9 KIDLINGTON, OXON Ballflower, *c* 1350
10 SOUTHWELL CATHEDRAL, NOTTS Naturalistic vine, *c* 1290
11 COGGES, OXON Four-petal flowers, *c* 1350

Perpendicular

12 OXFORD CATHEDRAL St. Frideswide's shrine.
13 WHITCHURCH, SOMERSET Stylised vine, *c* 1480
14 ST ALBANS CATHEDRAL, HERTS Stylised leaves and flowers, *c* 1

Wall Arcading

1 BRISTOL CATHEDRAL
Chapter House. Late Norman interlacing blind
arcading above seat-niches
2 LINCOLN CATHEDRAL
St Hugh's Choir. Early English 'Perspective'
double arcading in south aisle

Gothic Sculptural Decoration

1 LONDON, WESTMINSTER ABBEY
Censing angel in tribune arcade spandrel, north
transept, *c* 1250–5
2 LINCOLN CATHEDRAL
Angel Choir. Trumpeting angel in triforium
spandrel, *c* 1260

3 SALLE, NORFOLK
Detail of west doorway, the spandrels carved with feathered angels, *c* 1410

4 CAMBRIDGE
King's College Chapel. Angel corbel in the choir, *c* 1450

Below
5 LONDON, WESTMINSTER ABBEY
Henry VII's Chapel. Part of the Angel frieze above the arcade, with Tudor rose, portcullis, and fleur-de-lis below crowns

Carved Bosses to Stone-Ribbed Vaulting

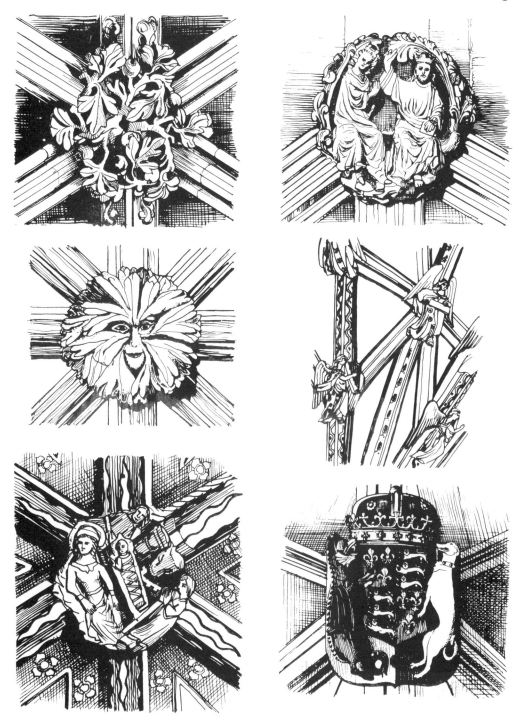

1 LINCOLN CATHEDRAL Angel Choir. Naturalistic hawthorn
2 LINCOLN CATHEDRAL Angel Choir. Coronation of the Virgin
3 NORWICH CATHEDRAL Cloisters. 'Green Man'
4 GLOUCESTER CATHEDRAL Choir. Angel musicians above high altar
5 TEWKESBURY ABBEY, GLOS Nativity
6 WINCHESTER CATHEDRAL, HANTS Royal Arms of Henry VII

Crockets and Corbels

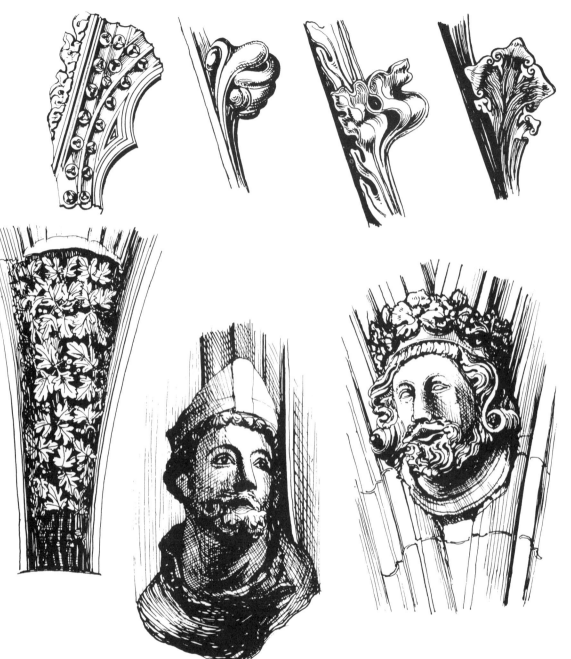

Top Row

1 OXFORD CATHEDRAL Part of a gabled and cusped arch, decorated with ballflower and leaf-crockets. Early Decorated

2 HEREFORD CATHEDRAL An early Decorated crocket

3 ST ALBANS CATHEDRAL, HERTS A Perpendicular crocket of stone

4 LITCHAM, NORFOLK All Saints Church. A Perpendicular crocket carved in wood, from the rood-screen

Bottom Row

5 EXETER CATHEDRAL, DEVON Naturalistic hazel and hawthorn corbel in choir arcade. Decorated, *c* 1300

6 ELY CATHEDRAL, CAMBS Corbel in the Octagon, portraying John of Hotham, made Bishop in 1316

7 ST ALBANS CATHEDRAL, HERTS Corbel portraying Edward II, south arcade of nave, rebuilt *c* 1323–5

1

4

2

5

3

1 SELBY ABBEY, YORKS Early English lavatory in the chapter house
2 CASTOR, NORTHANTS St Kyneburgha's Church. Late Norman double sedilia, and Early English
   double piscina
3 HAMBLEDON, BUCKS St Mary's Church. The Decorated (curvilinear) piscina and triple sedilia
4 BLEWBURY, BERKS St Michael's Church. The late Decorated squinch
5 YATTON, SOMERSET St Mary's Church. A rich Decorated piscina, canopied and standing on a
   pedestal-shaft

Medieval Furnishings
Norman Fonts

1 LINCOLN CATHEDRAL
The great font of black Tournai marble, one of ten similar examples in England. The square bowl, its sides boldly carved with grotesque animals, is supported by a massive central column and four detached shafts

2 DORCHESTER ABBEY, OXON
The superb lead font is decorated with seated figures of saints, framed in arches rising from twisted columns

Gothic Fonts

1 BARNACK, NORTHANTS
St John's Church contains an Early English stone font, its octagonal bowl resting on a stout central shaft surrounded by trefoiled arcading

2 SEETHING, NORFOLK
St Margaret's Church. The stone Perpendicular font has niched figures against the stem, and the sides of the octagonal bowl are carved with the Baptism of Christ and the Seven Sacraments

3 HUTTOFT, LINCS
St Margaret's Church. The stone Perpendicular font is richly carved, with the Signs of the Evangelists against the foot, saints against the stem, and winged angels below the octagonal bowl, the sides of which portray the Virgin, the Trinity, and the Apostles

Pulpits

1 BEAULIEU, HANTS
St Bartholomew's Church was formerly the abbey refectory, and it contains a uniquely beautiful Early English pulpit of semi-octagonal form projecting from an arch and reached by way of an arcaded wall-passage

2 COMBE, OXON
St Lawrence's Church contains a fine
Perpendicular pulpit of tracery-
panelled stonework, crested with
miniature battlements

3 CIRENCESTER, GLOS
St John's Church. The 'wineglass'
pulpit of rich Perpendicular tracery,
partly perforated

Carved Wooden Bench-Ends, etc.

1 NOSELEY, LEICS
St Mary's Church. This superb bench-end of *c* 1473 is carved with a roundel, containing a flower vase and three cockerels, below the ogee-headed frame with its rich poppy-head. The large cockerel at the side is the emblem of the Staunton family of Noseley

2 CHESTER CATHEDRAL
The choir is furnished with superb late Gothic choir-stalls. The side of the former abbot's stall is richly carved with a Tree of Jesse

Carved Stone Gargoyles

1 YORK MINSTER
South aisle of nave
2 PATRINGTON, YORKS
St Patrick's Church
3 YORK MINSTER
North aisle of choir

Carved Misericords, etc.

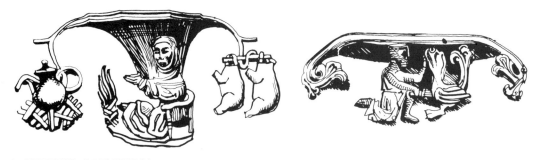

1 CHESTER CATHEDRAL
Choir. Misericord representing 'Winter'
2 EXETER CATHEDRAL
Choir. Misericord representing a knight slaying a dragon

Various Stone Carvings

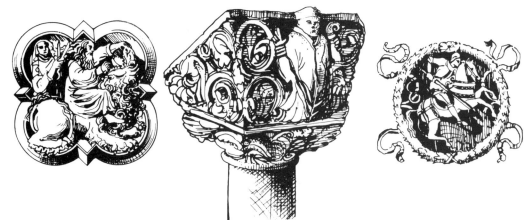

1 YORK MINSTER
South-west door of nave. Fourteenth century carved quatrefoil relief portraying Samson and Delilah
2 NORTON, WORCS
St Egwin's Church. Carved limestone lectern of late twelfth century date, from Evesham Abbey
3 LONDON
Southwark Cathedral. 1914–18 War Memorial by Sir Ninian Comper

Early Stuart and Commonwealth Churches

1 LEEDS, YORKS
St John's Church, built in 1632 by a local worthy, John Harrison, is a twin-vessel structure with a west tower. Designed in a simple Perpendicular style, it is an interesting example of Gothic survival

3–4 STAUNTON HAROLD, LEICS
Holy Trinity Church. Built in 1653–5 as a gesture of Anglican defiance to Commonwealth Puritanism, this private chapel was designed in the form a small parish church, with a west tower, an aisled and clerestoried nave of three bays, and an aisleless chancel. Except for the elaborate Jacobean Renaissance frontispiece framing the west door, the exterior is convincingly Perpendicular in style and spirit

Left
2 BERWICK, NORTHUMBERLAND
Holy Trinity Church, although built in 1648–52 by the Cromwellian governor Colonel Fenwicke, closely resembles St Katherine Cree, London, both inside and out. Its Laudian combination of Gothic and Renaissance features was almost certainly due to the employment of a London mason

5 LONDON, ST KATHERINE CREE
This church, rebuilt *c* 1628 under Laud's direct influence, is a sophisticated attempt to link the past and present by combining Gothic and Renaissance features. Thus, the Italian Renaissance arcades are surmounted by a late Gothic clerestory, and the ceilings are simulated ribbed vaults executed in plasterwork

6 LEEDS, YORKS
St John's Church. Like the exterior, the twin-nave interior is Perpendicular Gothic in style, but it is most sumptuously furnished with Jacobean Renaissance woodwork

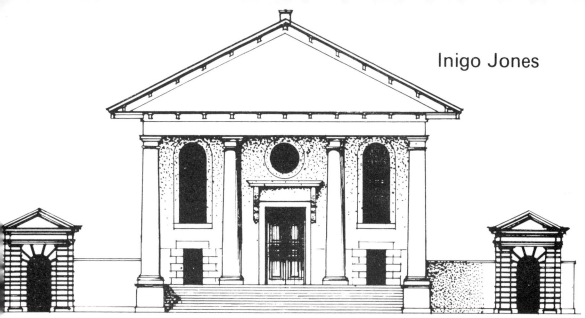

Inigo Jones

7 LONDON, ST PAUL'S, COVENT GARDEN
A complete break with the traditional forms of church-building was made in 1631, when Inigo Jones cast this estate chapel in the mould of an antique Tuscan temple, its bold tetrastyle portico derived through Palladio from Vitruvius

8 LONDON, OLD ST PAUL'S CATHEDRAL
Jones's external re-edification of the early Norman nave and transepts was carried out in an austerely simple 'Roman' style, although the west front was adorned with a magnificent Corinthian portico, in its time the finest north of the Alps

Late Stuart and Georgian Churches
Sir Christopher Wren

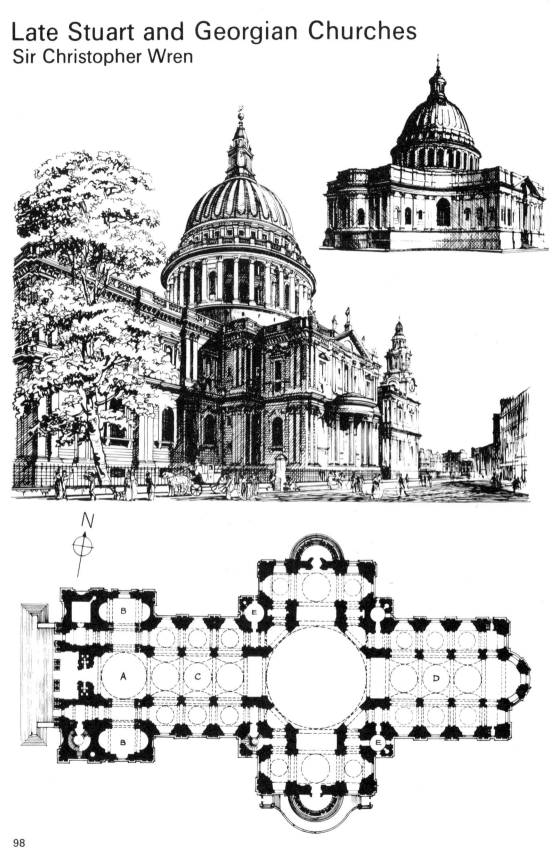

1–5 (p.100) LONDON, ST PAUL'S CATHEDRAL
The Greek Cross plan was developed in the Great
Model design by adding to the western arm a
large domed vestibule and a deep portico. The
executed plan, developed from that of the
Warrant Design, is a Latin cross with the four
main vessels and their aisles converging on an
octagonal central space. In the Warrant Design
this was virtually a Renaissance version of Ely's
Gothic octagon, with eight arches groined into a
low saucer-dome, its wide oculus opening to a
tall eight-windowed lantern with a
hemispherical dome, crowned externally by a
pagoda-like spire. The arms of the cross were to
have elevations closely resembling those of the
old cathedral as remodelled by Inigo Jones

The transverse section shows Wren's skill in
reconciling the inner dome, perfectly related to the
interior of the central space, with an outer dome
high enough to dominate the exterior. The
tapered inner drum, its Corinthian order skilfully
treated in perspective, supports the
hemispherical inner dome as well as a tall brick
cone on which rests the timber framework of the
outer dome and the stonework of the lantern

6–7 LONDON, ST STEPHEN'S, WALLBROOK

Built 1672–3, externally unimpressive but with
Wren's finest church interior. Within an oblong
body, sixteen Corinthian columns are arranged to
form a nave, having wide inner and narrow outer
aisles, subtly combined with a square central
space covered by a saucer-dome on eight
pendentives

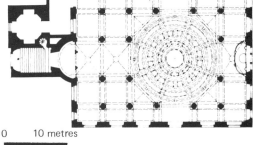

0   10 metres

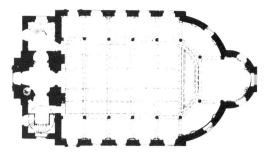

8 LONDON, ST CLEMENT DANES, STRAND
Built 1680–2, this large aisled and galleried basilica ends east in a trilobed apse, ingeniously planned to conform with the site's south boundary

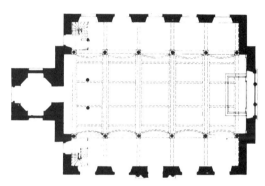

9 LONDON, ST JAMES'S, PICCADILLY
Built 1682–4 in an open churchyard. Regarded by Wren as his most perfect auditorium church, this aisled and galleried basilica was capable of seating some 2,000 worshippers, all within sight and sound of the altar and preacher

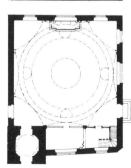

10–11 LONDON, ST MARY ABCHURCH
Built 1681–6, this square-bodied church is ceiled with a large saucer-dome on eight pendentives. The very fine furnishings include a splendid reredos with carvings by Grinling Gibbons

12–13 LONDON, ST MARTIN'S, LUDGATE HILL
Built 1677–84 and planned as a barrel-vaulted cross within a square. This church is entered on the south side through a three-bay vestibule, the middle bay forming the base of the tower. This is finished with an elegant ogee cupola and slender spire of leadwork, skilfully related to the dome and campanili of St Paul's

14 LONDON, ST MARY-LE-BOW, CHEAPSIDE

The famous steeple, completed 1680, begins with a massive square tower of two lofty stages. The lower has two exposed faces with a large rusticated arch framing a Doric doorway, and each face of the belfry stage has a divided arch framed by an Ionic order with paired pilasters. The balustrade extends between angle pinnacles formed of grouped consoles, and surrounds the spire. This consists of a circular Corinthian peristyle surmounted by a ring of inverted consoles which support a cruciform stage and an obelisk

Left

15 LONDON, ST BRIDE'S, FLEET STREET

This beautiful steeple was completed in 1703 with a 'spire' composed of four open-arched octagonal stages, each dressed with an appropriate order of pilasters and proportionately reduced in size. A cruciform obelisk rises from the top stage

Right

16 LONDON, ST VEDAST'S, FOSTER LANE

Wren's most Baroque steeple was completed in 1696 with a 'spire' of two stages. The lower and large one has four concave faces between Composite-pilastered angles, whereas the upper stage is circular with angle buttresses projecting to carry inverted consoles which rise against the crowning obelisk

17 LONDON, CHRIST CHURCH, NEWGATE STREET

The tower, completed 1704, finishes with a belfry stage dressed with a Doric order of pilasters, dividing each face into three narrow openings below a high segmental-pedimented attic. The 'spire' has a tall square stage with an Ionic peristyle above a high plinth. Above this temple-like stage rises a tall and narrow square shaft, having an open arch in each face, and an urn-finial

Far Right

18 LONDON, ST MAGNUS, LOWER THAMES STREET

Completed 1705, the square tower of this fine steeple has a belfry stage containing, in each face, an arched opening framed by paired Corinthian pilasters. Above a parapet of open arcading rises a tall octagonal lantern, dressed with an order of Corinthian pilasters and having an open arch in each face. The lead-covered dome is surmounted by a slender spirelet

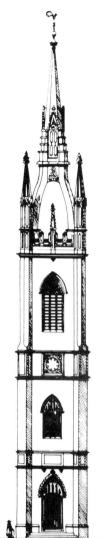

19 LONDON, ST DUNSTAN'S-IN-THE-EAST
Wren's elegant Gothic steeple, built 1697–9, finishes with a bow, or corona, formed by four flying buttresses rising diagonally behind the angle pinnacles and meeting to support a slender spirelet

21 LONDON, ST MARY ALDERMARY, BOW LANE
Rebuilt 1670–6, on its original plan, this handsome church is Wren's most considerable achievement in the Gothic or 'Saracenic' style, here enlivened with some Baroque details. The aisles and lofty clerestoried nave are finished alike with plaster vaulting formed with Perpendicular fans surrounding saucer-domes

20 LONDON, ST EDMUND'S, LOMBARD STREET
This church, built c 1670, has a charming front of three bays, the side ones finished with concave-profiled buttresses flanking the central tower which is surmounted by an octagonal lantern and a spire of slightly concave form, timber-framed and lead-covered

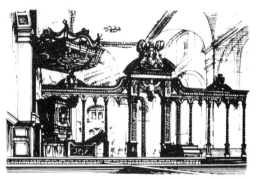

22 LONDON, ALL HALLOWS, UPPER THAMES STREET
This church, demolished 1893, was richly furnished with fine woodwork. The handsome arcaded screen, a rarity in Wren's City churches, and the pulpit-type are now in St Margaret's, Lothbury

103

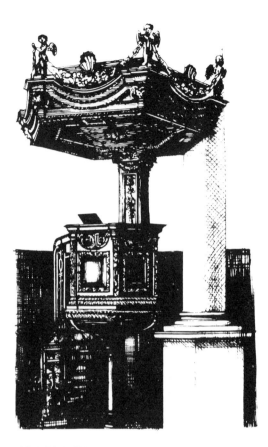

23 LONDON, ST STEPHEN'S, WALLBROOK
The finely-carved oak pulpit with its type, or sounding-board, decked with cherubs holding garlands

24 LONDON, ST PAUL'S CATHEDRAL
A part of the magnificent choir stalls, with the Bishop's Throne, the oak joinery decorated with superb carvings by Grinling Gibbons and his assistants

25–26 INGESTRE, STAFFS

The sumptuous parish church of St Mary, built 1673–6, was almost certainly designed by Wren. The nave arcade's arches rest on compound piers of four Doric columns, and above the plain clerestory of round windows is a flat ceiling richly modelled with plasterwork. The segmental ceiling of the aisleless chancel is similarly adorned

Baroque Churches
Thomas Archer

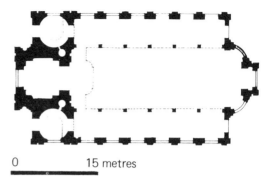

0   15 metres

27–30 BIRMINGHAM, ST PHILIP'S
Thomas Archer's first church, built 1709–15,
combines a fairly conventional galleried basilican
plan with Doric-pilastered elevations of Roman
Baroque grandeur. The superb concave-faced and
dome-crowned west tower, as well as the
pedimented doorways and oval windows above
them, show a first hand knowledge of
Borromini's works. The interior is also very
impressive, with fluted square-shafted Doric
columns supporting the nave arcade's arches, and
a giant Corinthian order dressing the sanctuary

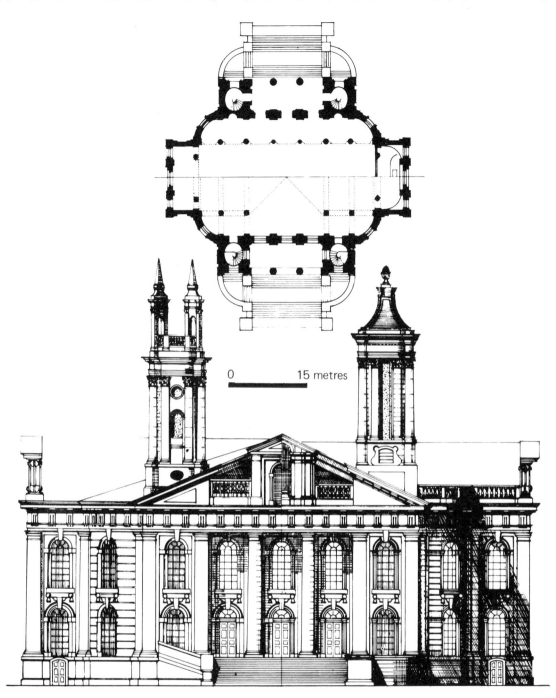

0   15 metres

31–32 LONDON, ST JOHN'S, SMITH SQUARE
Archer's most remarkable church, built 1712–30,
was planned as a wide-armed cross within an
oblong body, its quadrant corners flanking east
and west projecting bays. The church is entered,
however, on the north and south sides through
great Doric porticos flanked by oval staircase
towers. The elevation shows how Archer's
original design (left) was altered without his
approval during building (right)

Nicholas Hawksmoor

33–34 LONDON, ST ANNE'S, LIMEHOUSE
Hawksmoor's powerful and sombre Baroque
style found eloquent expression in his three
Stepney churches. St Anne's, built 1712–14, was
planned as a wide armed cross within an oblong
body. The exterior is dominated by the lofty west
tower, with its projecting semi-domed apse, its
diagonally-placed lantern stage, and its flanking
wings resembling transepts

35–36 LONDON, ST GEORGE'S, BLOOMSBURY

In this remarkable church, built 1720–30, Hawksmoor's Baroque imagination was coupled with his interest in antique monuments, finding expression in the noble 'Pantheon' portico and the terminal feature of the west tower, inspired by the Mausoleum at Halicarnassos

37 LONDON, CHRIST CHURCH, SPITALFIELDS

One of Hawksmoor's most striking works, this combination of Tuscan portico, tower-façade and obelisk spire was evolved only when the church was nearing completion around 1729

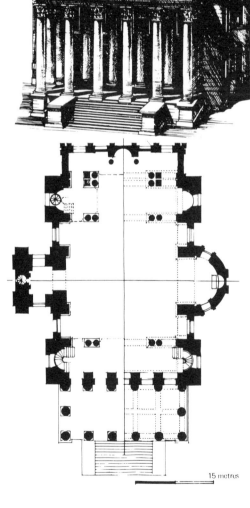

15 metres

Churches by James Gibbs, or Influenced by Him

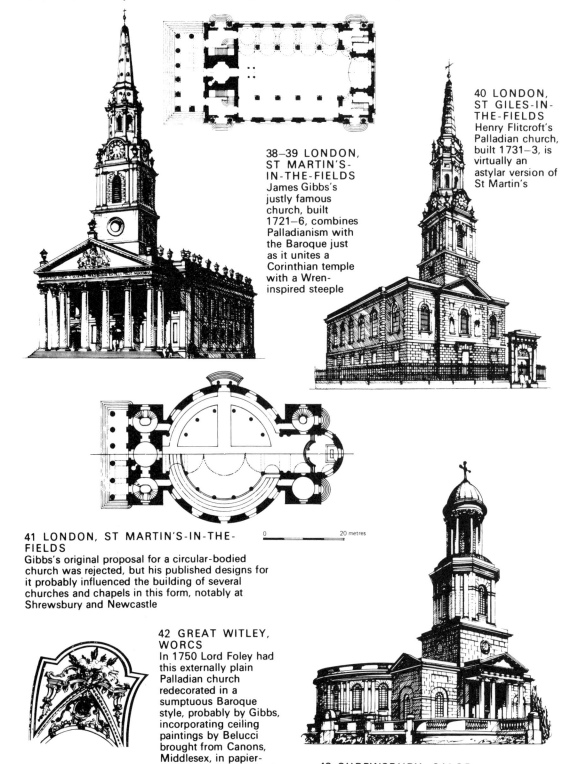

40 LONDON, ST GILES-IN-THE-FIELDS Henry Flitcroft's Palladian church, built 1731–3, is virtually an astylar version of St Martin's

38–39 LONDON, ST MARTIN'S-IN-THE-FIELDS James Gibbs's justly famous church, built 1721–6, combines Palladianism with the Baroque just as it unites a Corinthian temple with a Wren-inspired steeple

41 LONDON, ST MARTIN'S-IN-THE-FIELDS Gibbs's original proposal for a circular-bodied church was rejected, but his published designs for it probably influenced the building of several churches and chapels in this form, notably at Shrewsbury and Newcastle

0   20 metres

42 GREAT WITLEY, WORCS In 1750 Lord Foley had this externally plain Palladian church redecorated in a sumptuous Baroque style, probably by Gibbs, incorporating ceiling paintings by Belucci brought from Canons, Middlesex, in papier-maché reproductions of their original stucco settings

43 SHREWSBURY, SALOP St Chad's, designed by George Steuart and built in 1790–2, is an imposing neo-Classical church built on a circular plan

44 WARWICK
The nave and transepts of St Mary's Church were rebuilt *c* 1700 by Sir William Wilson, a mason-architect who followed Laudian precedent by using a curious but effective mixture of Gothic and Renaissance features. The imposing west tower, rising in three lofty stages above an open porch, has an elaborate finish recalling in outline the coronal of Gloucester's tower

45 MERE-WORTH, KENT
St Mary's Church, built *c* 1740, is a plain Tuscan temple with a semicircular portico and, surprisingly, a tall richly-decorated steeple deriving from Gibbs

46 SHEARSBY, LEICS
St Mary Magdalene's tower was rebuilt *c* 1790 to a design combining Palladian and Gothic features in a naive but charming manner

47 GALBY, LEICS
The nave and west tower of St Peter's Church were rebuilt *c* 1741 by a 'Mr Wing'. He employed a simple but fairly correct Perpendicular style for the nave, but crowned a 'Roman' west tower with four tall pagoda-like pinnacles flanking four low obelisks

Georgian Gothic

**48 SHOBDEN,
HEREFORDS**
St John's Church, built *c* 1753,
for the second Viscount
Bateman, has a charming
Rococo-Gothic interior
complete with its original
furnishings

49 TETBURY, GLOS
St Mary's, rebuilt 1777–81 by
Francis Hiorne of Warwick, is
outstanding among Georgian
Gothic churches, a vast and
lofty oblong hall divided into a
wide nave and galleried aisles
by two rows of extremely tall
and slender eight-shafted
columns, rising to support the
simple ribbed vaulting of
plasterwork

Later Georgian Churches

50–51 MISTLEY, ESSEX
In 1776 Robert Adam transformed a plain oblong
preaching-box into a most elegant neo-Classical
church. On each side he added an exedra-
transept and an entrance portico, and at either
end he built matching towers, their square shafts
surmounted by circular lanterns with domes.
These towers alone survive

0   50 metres

**52 LONDON, ST
JOHN'S, BETHNAL
GREEN**
Was built in 1826 and is
externally the most
remarkable of Sir John
Soane's 'Commissioners
Churches', a simple but
extremely subtle design
in his very personal neo-
Classical style, built in
yellow brick and
Portland stone

E.C.A.—H

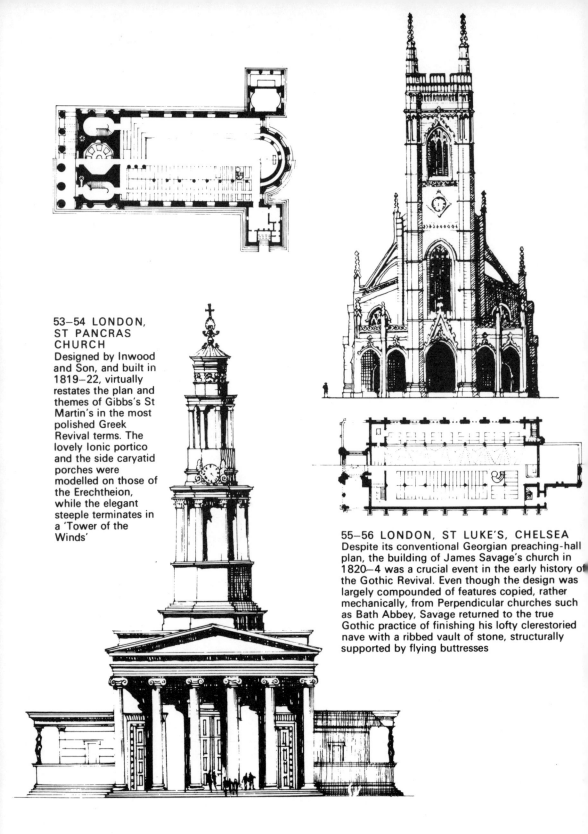

53–54 LONDON, ST PANCRAS CHURCH
Designed by Inwood and Son, and built in 1819–22, virtually restates the plan and themes of Gibbs's St Martin's in the most polished Greek Revival terms. The lovely Ionic portico and the side caryatid porches were modelled on those of the Erechtheion, while the elegant steeple terminates in a 'Tower of the Winds'

55–56 LONDON, ST LUKE'S, CHELSEA
Despite its conventional Georgian preaching-hall plan, the building of James Savage's church in 1820–4 was a crucial event in the early history of the Gothic Revival. Even though the design was largely compounded of features copied, rather mechanically, from Perpendicular churches such as Bath Abbey, Savage returned to the true Gothic practice of finishing his lofty clerestoried nave with a ribbed vault of stone, structurally supported by flying buttresses

Gothic Revival Churches: Exteriors

1 BRIGHTON, ST PETER'S CHURCH
Was designed in the Perpendicular style by Sir Charles Barry and built in 1823–8. The finely composed porch and tower, of white Portland stone, effectively close the tree-lined vista along the Steyne

Left
2 LEEDS, ST SAVIOUR'S
Was built in 1840–5 for Dr E.B. Pusey to bring Christian Light into the dark slums of 'The Bank'. Cruciform in plan, and Decorated Gothic in style, the church never received the rich garnishing of pinnacles and lofty central spire designed by J.M. Derick, its architect

3 BRIGHTON, ST PAUL'S CHURCH
Built 1846–8, was designed by R.C. Carpenter, an architect much favoured by the Camden Society. The east elevation shows the large Decorated geometrical-traceried window, containing glass by Pugin and lighting the chancel. The projected spire, 283 feet high, was abandoned and the tower was completed with an octagonal lantern of wood and leadwork by the architect's son, R.A Carpenter

4 LONDON, ST MARY MAGDALENE'S, PADDINGTON
In this striking church, built 1868–78, George Edmund Street showed his genius for uniting the Gothic styles of Europe by combining Early English and French motifs with the brick and stone mixtures of Italy and Germany

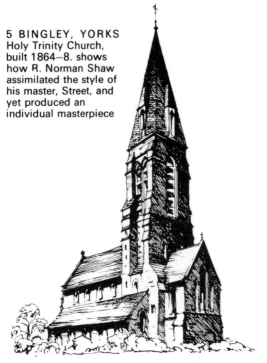

5 BINGLEY, YORKS
Holy Trinity Church,
built 1864—8. shows
how R. Norman Shaw
assimilated the style of
his master, Street, and
yet produced an
individual masterpiece

6 BRIGHTON, ST BARTHOLOMEW'S
Designed by Edmund Scott and built 1872—4,
this noble church rises above the surrounding
houses like a giant Gothic ark of polychromatic
brickwork, a monument to the piety and
generosity of its founder, Father Arthur Wagner

7 LONDON, ST AUGUSTINE'S, KILBURN
Built 1872—4, this great church is John
Loughborough Pearson's masterpiece. The finely
composed exterior is dominated by the great
plate-tracery rose window recessed in the west
front, and by the superb north-west steeple with
its broach spire

Gothic Revival Churches: Interiors

1 OMBERSLEY, WORCS
In St Andrew's Church, built 1825–9, Thomas Rickman made a brave attempt to create the effect of a truly Gothic interior, despite his use of plaster vaulting and the retention of side galleries, here skilfully recessed well back from the nave arcades

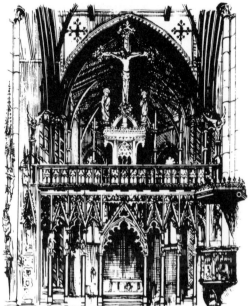

2 BIRMINGHAM, ST CHAD'S (RC) CATHEDRAL
Built 1839–41 with limited funds, the architectural shortcomings of this early work by A. W. N. Pugin are redeemed by the medieval splendour of the rood-screen

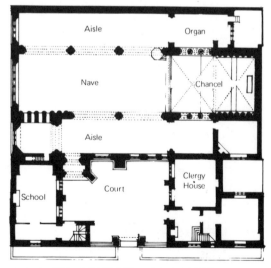

3 RAMSGATE, ST AUGUSTINE'S (RC) CHURCH
Built by Pugin in 1845–50, at his own expense, this very beautiful and honestly constructed church fully demonstrates his belief in 'The True Principles of Pointed or Christian Architecture'

4–5 (p.118) LONDON, ALL SAINTS, MARGARET STREET
Built 1850–9, William Butterfield's extraordinary masterpiece is essentially an early Decorated design carried out in 'constructional polychromy' of Italian Gothic inspiration

6 LONDON, ST COLUMBA'S, SHOREDITCH

The austerely beautiful interior of this brick-and-stone church, built 1867–71, is typical of what W.R. Lethaby described as James Brooks's 'big-boned' Gothic style

Below

7 LONDON, ST MARY MAGDALENE'S, PADDINGTON

Inside this church, built 1868–78, G.E. Street honestly and successfully differentiated the nave arcade opening to the wide 'south' aisle from that opening to the 'north' ambulatory passage, reconciling both by placing canopied figures in all the spandrels

8 BRIGHTON, ST BARTHOLOMEW'S

The almost Cistercian austerity of this lofty brick-built interior by Edmund Scott is enhanced by the splendour of the high altar and its setting, designed by Henry Wilson in *c* 1900

9 LONDON, ST AUGUSTINE'S, KILBURN
The magnificent interior of this church by J.L.
Pearson, probably inspired by that of Albi
Cathedral, France, is entirely covered with stone-
ribbed brick vaulting supported by lateral
buttresses which are pierced with openings
linking the bays of the inner aisle and the gallery

10 BRIGHTON, ST MICHAEL'S
The lofty nave has a simple exterior of red brick,
designed to accord with the earlier building by
G.F. Bodley, but the stone interior is a
magnificent example of William Burges's
vigorous style, inspired by early French Gothic
churches

Twentieth Century Churches

2 LONDON, ST SAVIOUR'S, ELTHAM
This brick-built church of 1933, designed by
Welch, Lander and Cachemaille-Day, is a boldly
expressive and simply detailed design showing
the influence of Dominikus Bohn, a contemporary
German church architect

1 WELLINGBOROUGH, NORTHANTS
The interior of St Mary's Church, begun 1906,
demonstrates most splendidly Sir Ninian Comper's
idea of 'Unity by Inclusion', with its lofty arcades
recalling those of Cotswold Perpendicular
churches, its elaborate fan and pendant vaulting
suggested by Oxford, and its wealth of richly
coloured and gilded screens and furnishings of
Renaissance inspiration

**3 ROKER,
YORKS**
Built 1907, of
undressed local
stone, St
Andrew's Church
is a striking
example of the
'Arts and Crafts'
Gothic style as
used by Edward S.
Prior. The
windows have
massive tracery of
a primitive
'Perpendicular'
character, and the
interior is
dominated by a
sequence of bold
unmoulded arches
rising from stumpy
columns

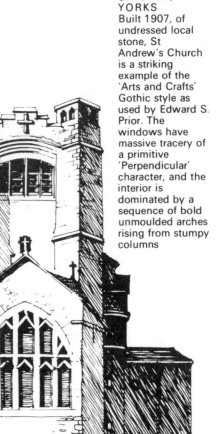

The New Cathedrals

Above
1 TRURO, CORNWALL
The last traditional Gothic cathedral, designed by
J. L. Pearson in 1880, is an accomplished essay
in the Early English style. It might be regarded as
a perfected version of Salisbury except for the
three tall spire-crowned towers, which reflect
Norman Gothic influence

2–3 LONDON, WESTMINSTER (RC) CATHEDRAL
John Francis Bentley was
commissioned in 1894 to design a
cathedral in a style other than his
favourite Gothic. Inspired by
Romano-Byzantine churches,
notably San Marco, Venice, he
created what Norman Shaw
described as 'the finest church that
has been built for centuries'. The
superbly proportioned brick
interior is being clothed, stage by
stage, with varied marbles and rich
mosaics

4 – 5 LIVERPOOL, ANGLICAN CATHEDRAL

Sir Giles Scott won the open competition for this great church in 1904. The most original feature is the plan, with a vast central space entered on either side through porches between shallow transepts. To the ritual east is a choir of three bays, balanced on the west by a nave, yet to be completed. Exterior and interior are huge in scale and simple in composition, with rich Flamboyant Gothic details skilfully related to large plain surfaces of red sandstone

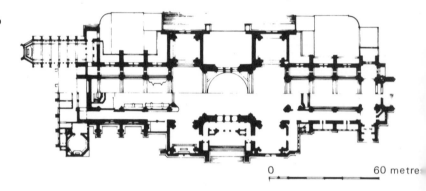

0   60 metres

6 – 8 COVENTRY, WARWICKS

The new Cathedral of St Michael, designed by Sir Basil Spence and built 1956–62, has attracted more interest than any other modern church. Designed in a contemporary idiom, it is virtually a hall-church having saw-toothed side walls and a lofty open porch linking it with the war-scarred ruins of the old cathedral. Within there is a cellular sounding-board ceiling upheld by two rows of extremely slender columns, like a modern version of Tetbury, much lovely stained glass, and Sutherland's great tapestry above the high altar

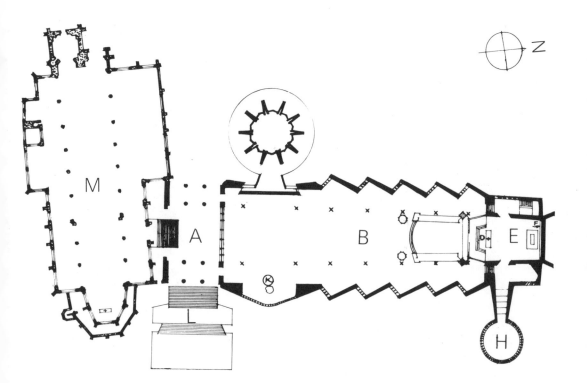

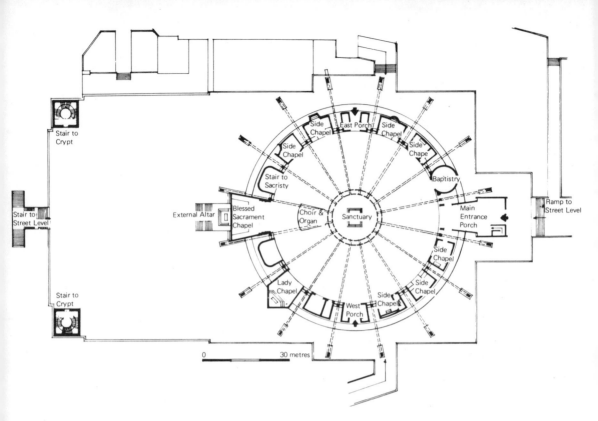

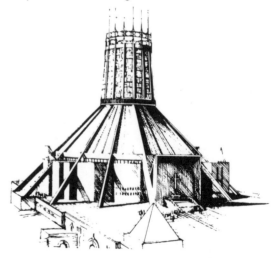

9 LIVERPOOL, THE ROMAN CATHOLIC CATHEDRAL

With a boldly original design, won in competition in 1965, Sir Frederick Gibberd's great concrete-framed 'cathedral in the round' appears to break completely with past church-building traditions, although such centrally-planned churches were a Renaissance ideal, and a prototype for its lantern-crowned conical form might be seen in Hurley's timber framing for Ely's Late Gothic octagon

Index

126